THE
EVERYTHING
COLLEGE
CHECKLIST
BOOK

The ultimate, all-in-one handbook for
getting in—and settling in—to college!

Cynthia C. Muchnick, MA

A adamsmedia

Avon, Massachusetts

*For Justin, Jacob, Ross, and Ally. May you find
rewarding college experiences of your own someday.
And to Adam, the greatest guy I met in college.*

An Everything® Series Book.
Everything® and everything.com® are registered trademarks of F+W Media, Inc.

Published by Adams Media, a division of F+W Media, Inc.
57 Littlefield Street, Avon, MA 02322. U.S.A.
www.adamsmedia.com

ISBN 10: 1-4405-4413-1
ISBN 13: 978-1-4405-4413-2
eISBN 10: 1-4405-4515-4
eISBN 13: 978-1-4405-4515-3

Printed in the United States of America.

10 9 8 7 6 5 4 3 2 1

Readers are urged to take all appropriate precautions before undertaking any how-to task. Always read and follow instructions and safety warnings for all tools and materials, and call in a professional if the task stretches your abilities too far. Although every effort has been made to provide the best possible information in this book, neither the publisher nor the author are responsible for accidents, injuries, or damage incurred as a result of tasks undertaken by readers. This book is not a substitute for professional services.

*This book is available at quantity discounts for bulk purchases.
For information, please call 1-800-289-0963.*

Contents

The Top 10 Things to Do During Your First Year of College. . .10

Introduction. 11

1. Choosing a College. 15

Information Sources 16

Campus Visits 18

Questions to Ask 20

Campus Visit Notes 21

Should You Stay or Should You Go?. 30

Who to Contact with Questions 32

Plan to Keep in Touch 34

2. Financing Your Education. 39

Financial Aid 101: Offices and Forms 40

Finding Scholarships and Grants 41

Leadership Development Awards. 45

Work-Study Aid and Other Jobs. 46

Loans 48

Cost Versus Value 50

Financial Aid Tracker 52

3. Preparations Before Heading to Campus. 57

Advice on Bills and Financial Materials 58

Health Insurance Basics 59

Safety and Your New Room or Apartment. 62

Housing How-Tos 63
Students with Disabilities. 66
Orientation 67

4. The Big Move **73**
Packing for a College Room 74
Bathroom Essentials and Medications 78
What to Wear 81
Making It Feel Like Home 84
Moving Out and Summer Storage 89

5. Roommates and Dorms **91**
Roommate Selection 92
Meet Your Roommate 93
Moving In. 99
Roommate Agreements. 101
Managing Conflicts 104

6. Personal Finance at College **109**
Cash, School Charge Card, Check, Debit, or Credit 110
Should You Get a Credit Card? 112
Finding a Local Bank 115
Balancing Your Checkbook 118
Living on a Budget 120

7. Keeping Clean. **125**
Keeping a Clean Room 126
Laundry Lessons 101. 128
Campus Laundry Services 133
Final Laundry Thoughts 133

8. Choosing Classes and a Major **135**
Advisement 136
Balance Your Schedule 138
Core Requirements 141
Declaring a Major 144
Minors and Double Majors 147
Studying Abroad 148

9. Time Management **157**
Create a Master Calendar 158
Trading Time Blocks 161
Combining Tasks 162
Planners and Calendars 164
Cramming Warning 166
Time Management Checklist 167

10. Effective Study Skills **169**
Taking Notes in Class 170
Organization Tips 172
Study Groups 174
Flash Cards 176
Effective Reading 177
Study Skills Summary 179

11. Researching Papers **181**
Conducting Research 182
Research Is a Process 184
Where to Find Possible Sources .185
Keeping Track of Sources 190
Taking Notes 191

Using Note Cards 193
Plagiarism 101 195

12. Writing a Paper 197
Plan Your Attack 198
Write the First Draft 201
The Structure of Your Paper 202
Polishing a Rough Draft 209
Proofread! Proofread! Proofread! 212

13. Internships and Summer Jobs 215
Meaningful Work 216
Internship Basics 217
Finding Internships 219
Reflections on Your Experience 226

Appendix A.
Internet Resources for College Students 229

Appendix B.
Strategic Timelines for Choosing a Major 239

Appendix C.
Internet Resources for Finding a Major 245

Index 249

Acknowledgments

Thank you to the following important people for your support and help in making this book possible: Grace Freedson, my literary agent, who finds me these exciting projects, and Lisa Laing and Brett Palana-Shanahan at Adams Media.

And to my dear friends and family near and far: Sarah Bancroft, Nancy Cutler, Vicky deFelice, Robin Glasser, Mollie Hudner-Thompson, Cynthia Jenkins, Lexi Kalikman, Kiko Korn, Frandy Laster, Keri Ueberroth, Megan Walters, Ziggy Silbert, my awesome sisters Karen Shea and Linda Rosen, and my amazing parents, Gloria and Jack Clumeck. And finally to Adam, Justin, Jacob, Ross, and Alexa who teach me something new each and every day.

The Top 10 Things to Do
During Your First Year of College

1. Get involved! Find an organization that interests you and attend meetings, plan events, and meet great new friends.

2. Invite a professor to the cafeteria for lunch. Getting to know professors as more than just teachers is a great opportunity.

3. Visit a new friend at his home. Travel to see a different part of the country, meet a new college friend's family, and enjoy the break from classes.

4. Bring a new friend home with you. Show off your hometown, introduce your new friend to your family and high school buddies, and enjoy a favorite home-cooked meal.

5. Get to know the library. Become acquainted with the campus library and e-library system early in your college career and you'll reap the benefits until the day you graduate.

6. Stay connected with your parents from time to time through text messages, Skype, phone calls, e-mail, or snail mail.

7. Find a favorite local restaurant. Eating out is a great way to relax with friends and recharge your battery.

8. Attend parties. Gather a group of friends to dance, play games, or just hang out. Find your place in the social scene and balance out your study stress.

9. Visit your high school teachers. Round up some friends, visit your old teachers, and tell them about college. Thank them for helping you get there.

10. Create (or revise) a resume. Get assistance from your school's career office and prepare a resume that will impress future prospective employers (including that all-important "summer job" employer!). Starting early will get you on the path to a great job after graduation.

Introduction

AFTER TWELVE YEARS OF formal education, the end is in sight. Yet in order to pursue your dreams and increase your earning potential, you are about to head to college. An undergraduate degree by itself means several more years of classes, papers, and tests. If you pursue a graduate degree, you could be in school for another six to ten years. And you are actually looking forward to this?

Of course you're looking forward to college! These will be the best years of your life so far. You will make lifelong friends and perhaps meet your soul mate. You will try new things, learn valuable skills, and be challenged to figure out who you really are and what you stand for. You will fall in love with some of your classes (and perhaps classmates), deeply discuss serious issues with peers and professors, and enjoy many moments of quiet reflection.

You have achieved a lot and have done well in order to graduate from high school. You have learned what teachers want and how to succeed. However, college classes will move faster and your professors will be more demanding. You'll read thousand of pages and process dense information for class discussions and presentations. You'll also write hundreds of pages in essays, reports, and exams. To do so, you will spend many hours researching in the library and online, as well as many more hours studying in your room, in quiet places around campus, and even in the cafeteria.

As you are working harder and becoming smarter, you will also be having more fun than ever before. There will be more concerts, parties, and cultural events than you have time to attend. You will have a full range of athletics to watch or participate in, a new local community to explore, nearby exercise facilities to work out in, and perhaps even natural resources such as hiking trails, beaches, or ski mountains to enjoy. You will meet and live with interesting people, some from places you have never visited, with very different backgrounds and experiences than yours. By developing these new friendships, you'll learn more about yourself and what you want out of life.

By the time you finish college, you'll be prepared for a job in a field that may become a career. You'll also be prepared to change jobs if necessary, and you will still have college resources available to help you make that change. Your education in the classroom will be represented by your degree, but your education outside of the classroom will shine on your resume and in job interviews. Leadership experiences, internships, and semesters spent abroad will all help shape your approach to life and your contribution to the adult world.

This book was written as a guide and plan for you, as an incoming college freshman, and for your family. The topics covered in the following chapters will help you think about and prepare for the remarkable experience that is college. Each student's experience is different, but the themes students encounter are very similar, no matter what the size or location of the college. With a little thought and preparation, the transition from living at home and attending high school to living on your own and attending college can be a smooth one.

The experiences you have at college, in and out of the classroom, will not only help you personally and professionally upon graduation, but will also help you determine your place in the world. The education and the great memories you leave with will be yours forever. Regardless of your background or future plans, you are about to embark on a priceless journey. Good luck, and enjoy every minute!

CHAPTER 1

Choosing a College

When deciding where to apply to college, take into consideration many factors such as location, cost, size, reputation, academic programs, and campus traditions. Choosing where you might want to spend the next four years of your life is an exciting and daunting process. While you may feel like you are on the outside looking in, devising a college list can be exciting and fun if you turn the process into a personal research project. Do your homework diligently and dig deep to learn all that you can about the campuses that may interest you. Your matches are definitely out there somewhere just waiting to be found!

Information Sources

There are many different sources of information you can consult about which college is best for you. Because the following sources do not all provide the same kind of information, you should consult several of them. The more information you have, the more well rounded the picture of the school you're researching will be. Following are a few resources to consult.

College Guides

There are almost as many college guides on the market as there are colleges. Many guides simply list basic facts about the schools, such as the number of students, the student-to-teacher ratio, requirements to graduate, majors offered, and average SAT scores of those admitted; while other guides are more subjective, trying to paint a portrait of life at the school and to elaborate on each school's strengths and weaknesses. Both kinds of books can be quite valuable, particularly in the early stages of your college search, when you are identifying a range of schools that are right for you. As you narrow down your choices, you can get more detailed information from other sources.

Websites

All colleges and universities have their own websites. Visit these sites and get a variety of information about a school. Check out online course catalogs, campus clubs and organizations, school traditions, and the student online newspaper, seeking any particular areas of interest to you. Your goal is to try to get a feel for the vibe of a campus without having visited. So dig deep and read student testimonials and any-thing that will give you the flavor and feel of a campus. There are also several online college guides, many provided by the same publishers as the college guide books you see in the bookstore.

College Brochures and Catalogs

You can write or e-mail specific schools and request information. Keep in mind that their brochures are designed to present the school in the best possible light. Essentially school-produced booklets and publications are public rela-tions pieces and advertisements. Still, the brochures will pro-vide important basic information. Additionally, peruse the online course catalog.

Essential

Visit Facebook or college blog posts to hear directly from cur-rent students what is on their minds. Also read different campus student newspapers online to get a better sense of the culture and flavor of the student body.

Friends and Relatives

Ask people where they went to school (or are currently going) and how they feel about it. Ask specific questions about assets and drawbacks. Keep in mind, though, that people are different. What one person may have loved or hated about the school may not affect you the same way. Be especially wary of the "Legacy Trap"—just because a close relative went to a particular school and loved it does not mean it's necessarily the best place for you. Consider your own interests and needs, and find a school that meets them.

Campus Visits

Visiting a school is an excellent way to get a tremendous amount of information about it. You'll see the campus the way it really looks, not as it appears in the fancy brochure photos. Go on a campus tour and check out the admissions office, where there is often some kind of information session for students.

Make sure you talk to students; they will give you an accurate assessment of the school from the student's point of view. If possible, arrange to stay overnight in a dormitory (most schools make this experience available to applicants). Of course, visiting schools is time-consuming and can be expensive; you should plan to visit only those schools you are seriously considering attending.

Before visiting a college, you should do a few things to prepare:

☐ Speak to your college counselor and high school teachers before you go in order to get your absences excused from your current school.

☐ Call or e-mail the college admissions office to find out times of campus tours, information sessions, and to schedule an interview (if applicable).

☐ Arrange for a room at a local hotel or perhaps an on-campus dorm room to stay in if the college allows this.

☐ Ask if you can visit any classes while on campus. Some schools allow visitors to sit in on certain classes when visiting. Others require you to be admitted before doing so.

☐ Prepare for your visit by reading over college literature, visiting the school website, checking out Facebook pages or blogs written by current students, etc., to get a more personalized flavor of the campus vibe.

☐ Make a list of questions to ask of current students, teachers, and admissions representatives about the concerns you have and to gather more information.

When you visit a campus, be sure to do the following:

☐ Take a guided tour.

☐ Visit the campus bookstore and get a souvenir.

☐ Eat in the cafeteria or a central campus dining hub. Eavesdrop on students and listen in to what they are talking about.

☐ Spend time in the library. Is it a good place to study? Check out the environment. You will likely be spending a lot of your time there.

☐ Read a campus newspaper to get current information on what is happening and to hear what is important to students.

☐ Check out a dorm room if allowed.

☐ Ask your tour guide "tough" questions such as why he/she chose the school or what he/she does not like about the school.

☐ Seek out faculty members on your own from specific departments that interest you.

☐ Visit the student activity center and look at the bulletin boards to see what is going on around campus.

☐ Ask to see the athletic facilities that interest you: fields, gymnasium, pool, courts, etc. Observe students using them and see what you think.

Finally, keep a notebook to log your campus visits. Note cool facts, traditions, campus tour highlights, e-mail addresses of current students you may have met, and names of interesting classes or professors you may have collected. You will refer back to these notes when it comes time to apply to college and may even use some of the content you gathered in your actual college application questions.

Questions to Ask

During the college visiting process, it's a good idea to prepare some questions to ask tour guides, admissions representatives, professors, and anyone else you might meet during your visit. Here are some basic questions you can start with:

• What distinguishes this college from others in the area?
• What campus tradition or annual event do you most enjoy?

- With what colleges do you see the greatest number of overlapping applications?
- What are the college's retention and graduation rates? Why do students choose to leave?
- What's the best academic experience you've had?
- What have been your most memorable classes? Which professor(s) should I try to study with before graduation?
- What did you do last Saturday night or last weekend? Was it pretty typical of what goes on around campus?
- What do you like the least about your college? What would you like to change about it?
- Why did you choose to come to this college? Where else were you accepted?
- What is the surrounding community like? Do students stay on campus mostly or visit local areas?
- How is the food?
- How is the housing?

Of course, you may have some more specific questions to ask, so add them to the list. Don't be shy—information gathering is your main goal as you visit colleges.

Campus Visit Notes

When you visit multiple schools, your memories of each might blur together. Use this list to keep track of information for each of your school visits. You might want to refer back to these notes when you revisit any colleges for a second look.

Name of College: _____

Date Visited: _____

Name/E-mail of People Spoken To: _____

_____

_____

_____

_____

_____

Overall Impression: _____

_____

_____

_____

_____

_____

Facilities: _____

_____

_____

_____

_____

_____

Academic Programs: _____

_____

_____

_____

_____

Special Features/Points of Interest: _____

_____

_____

_____

_____

_____

Location/Environment: _____

_____

_____

_____

_____

_____

Campus Traditions: _____

_____

_____

_____

_____

_____

Other Details to Remember: _____

_____

_____

_____

_____

_____

_____

_____

Name of College: _____

Date Visited: _____

Name/E-mail of People Spoken To: _____

_____

_____

_____

_____

_____

Overall Impression: _____

_____

_____

_____

_____

_____

Facilities: _____

_____

_____

_____

_____

_____

Academic Programs: _____

_____

_____

_____

_____

Special Features/Points of Interest: _____

_____

_____

_____

_____

_____

Location/Environment: _____

_____

_____

_____

_____

_____

Campus Traditions: _____

_____

_____

_____

_____

_____

Other Details to Remember: _____

_____

_____

_____

_____

_____

_____

Name of College: _____

Date Visited: _____

Name/E-mail of People Spoken To: _____

_____

_____

_____

_____

_____

Overall Impression: _____

_____

_____

_____

_____

_____

Facilities: _____

_____

_____

_____

_____

_____

Academic Programs: _____

_____

_____

_____

_____

Special Features/Points of Interest: _____

_____

_____

_____

_____

_____

Location/Environment: _____

_____

_____

_____

_____

_____

Campus Traditions: _____

_____

_____

_____

_____

_____

Other Details to Remember: _____

_____

_____

_____

_____

_____

_____

Name of College: _____

Date Visited: _____

Name/E-mail of People Spoken To: _____

_____

_____

_____

_____

_____

Overall Impression: _____

_____

_____

_____

_____

_____

Facilities: _____

_____

_____

_____

_____

_____

Academic Programs: _____

_____

_____

_____

_____

Special Features/Points of Interest: _____

_____

_____

_____

_____

_____

Location/Environment: _____

_____

_____

_____

_____

_____

Campus Traditions: _____

_____

_____

_____

_____

_____

Other Details to Remember: _____

_____

_____

_____

_____

_____

_____

Should You Stay or Should You Go?

You may be choosing between a college that is closer to home or in your same geographical region, or one that is far away, more than just a drive. Here are some pros and cons to add to your own list of factors you may be weighing.

THE PROS FOR ATTENDING COLLEGE CLOSE TO HOME

- You are used to the weather and the general environment is familiar.
- You may have local lifelong friends also attending college close to home.
- You can bring home your laundry from time to time.
- You can set up your room over time, bringing items from home as you see fit or sending items back that don't work in your room.
- You can have a home-cooked meal from time to time.

THE CONS FOR ATTENDING COLLEGE CLOSE TO HOME

- You may want more space from your high school or local friends
- You may want more space from your parents
- It's too close to home!
- College may feel like just an extension of high school with more of the same routines continuing in your life. For example, you may feel that you are not experiencing

the independence of being far from home or missing out on the opportunities to have unfamiliar experiences in a new place.

✅ Fact

Take time to tour college campuses, whether they are schools you will apply to or not. It is important to see what your goal is in doing this "job" called high school. Any time you are traveling near a college campus, even if it is close to home, take a tour, visit the bookstore, and ask current students lots of questions to get a feel for the campus culture. Don't be shy!

THE PROS FOR GOING FAR AWAY FOR COLLEGE

- You get to reinvent yourself and start the year with a clean slate and no reputation to follow you.
- You get to experience a new city, town, or geographical region complete with new weather, new traditions, and a more diverse mixture of people.
- You get to spend four years away from home and then decide if you want to come back or not after college!
- You may feel more independent not having your family as a safety net so close by.

THE CONS FOR GOING FAR AWAY FOR COLLEGE

- Homesickness!
- The cost of travel and time it takes to get to your school may weigh on you over time.
- Your parents and childhood friends are geographically far away.

Who to Contact with Questions

Colleges put a lot of effort into making their communications self-explanatory and complete. But they also know that this is your first time through the process and some things may not make sense to you initially. From time to time, you may have a question not answered in the materials that you receive, or what you receive may only confuse you. The quickest and easiest way to get the information you need is to call or e-mail someone at the college. Make sure you reach out to staff people working in the following offices via e-mail or phone when seeking answers to specific questions.

- The admissions office (and your application confirmations from them) allows you to track that all parts of the application have arrived
- The health services office assists with your health forms and specific issues like allergies or accessibility of mental health services that you may need
- The housing office informs you about types of rooms, housing options, meal plans, etc.

- Specific coaches or the athletic department assists with recruiting questions, athletic admission concerns and academic support pertaining to athletes.

Other people and places to contact are suggested here:

1. Call or e-mail the office that sent you the information that created the question. If you have a question about your bill, call the number or e-mail the address listed at the top or bottom of your bill. If you have a question about health insurance forms, contact the health center. These offices probably hear your particular question regularly and can provide you with a quick answer.
2. If your question isn't obviously attached to a particular office, there are two places to contact. The orientation office can usually field a wide variety of new-student questions. If they're not able to answer your question, they can usually connect you with the correct office. Not only are they expecting most contacts to be questions from new students, they are cheerful and eager to be helpful.
3. Contact the tour guide who took you around campus or any current students you may know or have met along the way if you have their phone numbers or e-mail addresses.
4. Contact any alumni you or your parents may know. While their perspectives may not be current, they do have unique insights (and hindsight) they can share.

Question

What if my first choice doesn't offer me enough aid to attend the college?
Contact your financial aid officer and ask if there is an appeal process. Some schools will consider offers you've received from other colleges or recent changes in your family's specific circumstances. Be warned that state and community colleges typically have little flexibility in their offers.

Plan to Keep in Touch

The few months before college are a great time to start thinking about all the people you want to stay in touch with while at college. While you will probably stay in contact with your friends and immediate family via texting or social networking sites, don't forget those important people in your life who are not connected electronically, such as, perhaps, your grandparents. Send them a card or letter every month or so to let them know how and what you are doing, and call them from time to time to let them know you care and to keep up with family news.

Transitioning and Letting Go

You will always be your parents' child, but as you become an adult, your relationship with them is going to change. While at college, you will still rely heavily on your parents for financial and emotional support. However, you will no longer depend on them for day-to-day help and you will have significantly less contact with them. If you are the first or last child in your family to go to college, this transition may be particularly difficult at first. Your parents will have to adjust to your absence and new independence, and you will need to find support in new places.

When you are about to leave for school, try to set some ground rules with your parents. Both you and your parents should try to come up with some arrangement that is mutually acceptable. Obviously once you are at college, some of these ground rules you set may change or shift depending on your schedules and changing needs. Discuss together the following questions or ideas:

- How often will you speak or communicate: daily, weekly, monthly?
- What method of communication works best for you all: phone, text, e-mail, Skype, iChat, or other?
- How often will you see one another? Can your parents come to campus unannounced (if you live closer to home)? Is it ever okay for them to surprise you? How often do you plan to come home?
- How will you communicate about finances and what is the best way to transfer money into your bank or school account?
- Should your mom or dad e-mail you helpful reminders about your laundry, suggestions on how to deal with school situations, or your level of communication with other

relatives (grandparents, siblings, etc.), or do you want to handle those on your own?

After you have been at college awhile, you will become accustomed to your new independence. Consequently, going home for a break, particularly an extended break, can be a bit of a shock to you and your parents. What will happen when you come home and live under their roof again?
Discuss these concerns:

- Do they expect you to follow the rules you had while in high school?
- Are you hoping to come and go as you please as you would at college?
- Do you think you should be able to keep your regular college hours (perhaps sleeping late and staying up late) or are you expected to fit back into the family schedule?
- Are you expected to attend family meals?
- Are you expected to return to family chores or obligations or are you now more of a "guest" in your home?

Before heading home for your first break, have an open discussion with your parents about what the expectations are. Some limits may still remain, but you should be able to negotiate a plan that works for everyone.

One thing you will quickly realize is just how smart your parents are. During high school you probably felt that you knew almost everything you needed to know, and your parents were a little out of touch. But by the time you finish your first semester of college, you will be amazed by how many important things your parents know about relationships, time management, budgeting, school work, and even having fun. This is the time for you to start engaging your parents as an adult child, through something more akin to friendship than a subordinate relationship. Share with them some of the things you are experiencing at college, and be open to hearing their thoughts and answering their questions. You may find that you really like your parents, even if you wouldn't choose to go back and live at home again.

CHAPTER 2

Financing Your Education

You have selected the schools you like most and have completed your applications. Though your acceptance letters and final decision may yet be months away, now is the time for you to figure out how you're going to pay for that college education. Few families have enough money to pay for a college education outright. You and your family will have to make some sacrifices, be a bit creative, and use a variety of methods to get the money needed to see you through several years of college. The following provides your basic course in Financial Aid 101.

Financial Aid 101: Offices and Forms

Your college's financial aid office will be one of the first to contact you after you are accepted to the school. The financial aid officers at your school have an excellent understanding of student needs, federal regulations, and the paperwork necessary to receive financial aid. They have heard every question imaginable and understand that each student's situation may be unique. Financial aid officers also know of helpful resources available to students, including many outside of the college.

Make sure you pay close attention to all communication from this office and be certain that you return all forms, filled out completely, by the deadlines indicated. Keep the financial aid office phone number and web address in your phone or laptop and try to communicate with the same person each time you make contact. Your financial aid officer will usually remember your past conversations and can thus more accurately answer your new questions.

A common misconception is that you must be either very smart or very poor in order to receive financial aid. This is not even close to the truth. A variety of aid options exist for students of all levels of academic achievement and economic status. Search diligently and you will find something designed for someone in your situation.

Here's what you need to do as you apply for financial aid:

1. **File Tax Returns Promptly.** The closer you file to January 1, the better, since state programs, which rely on information provided in the FAFSA, are first come, first served. When the financial aid dollars are all allocated, the money is gone.

2. **Provide Tax Returns.** Provide your school with a signed copy of your tax return, as well as your parents' tax returns. If your parents are separated or you have other special circumstances, get in touch with your financial aid officer to find out what forms are needed from each person

3. **Complete the FAFSA.** The Free Application for Federal Student Aid (FAFSA) should be completed online early in the calendar year. The FAFSA form standardizes much of the information colleges use to determine a student's expected family contribution and need.

4. **Keep Track of Paperwork.** Every aid application will require paperwork. Be certain that you keep copies of all the forms you fill out so that you can refer to them later. Keeping applications in separate paper or computer folders may help you find items quickly when you are on the phone asking questions or trying to figure out how much aid you have secured.

Finding Scholarships and Grants

Scholarships and grants are defined amounts of money that the college or another source gives to you for your educational expenses; these don't have to be repaid. Scholarships are the most sought-after type of aid for most college students. Scholarship eligibility is normally based on student characteristics, including one's academic merit, declared major, alumni relationship, and extracurricular involvement.

Grants are different in that eligibility is usually based on the financial need of the student and family. Institutional grants are more common at private colleges than at public institutions. The federal government is probably the largest single source of financial aid for college students, typically focusing on need-based grants.

How to Obtain Scholarships

There are thousands of scholarships, small and large, out there. You may find that there is a scholarship for students living in your geographic region, planning to pursue your major, or pursuing any number of other special interests. Or maybe there is one for people with your ethnic background or even with your last name! Here are some places to find them:

- ☐ Online search engines (search for "college scholarships")
- ☐ Scholarship sites, like *www.guaranteed-scholarships.com* or *www.college-scholarships.com*
- ☐ Private organizations and local businesses in your community
- ☐ Community-based service groups, such as the Rotary Club, Elks Club, Lions Club, 4H, Veterans of Foreign Wars (VFW), and others
- ☐ Community agencies, such as churches and civic groups
- ☐ Your family's employers may have grant programs for children or dependents of employees
- ☐ Scholarship databases, like *www.fastweb.com* or *www .freSchinfo.com*. (Be cautious about any organizations that charge for their services. Some groups will try to sell you a list or have you complete an application so

that you can be included in a database. Your search should not require either activity.)

☐ Find out what types of scholarships your school offers. Some high schools have well-coordinated processes in place for applying for local scholarships, followed by an "awards night" of some sort, so be sure to check with your school counselor who may also be a great resource for local scholarship sources

☐ If you work for a national chain store or restaurant, ask about employee scholarships

Don't be shy about your involvement and accomplishments when searching for financial aid. You are your own best promoter, and you need to talk about your qualifications confidently. Include positions you've held, groups you have been a member of, and any community service you have done. Be confident in your approach and truthful about your qualifications.

🔔 Alert

Each year hundreds of thousands of dollars in college scholarship money is left unawarded due to a lack of applications. There are scholarships for almost every activity and interest; research scholarships online or at your library and apply for every scholarship you qualify for.

Your goal is to gain as much grant, scholarship, and award support as possible, even if it means getting a lot of small awards. You must notify your college financial aid office of any scholarships or grants that you obtain from outside sources. Be certain to ask your financial aid officer how outside scholarships and grants will affect your overall package.

Maintaining Grants and Scholarships

Getting grants and scholarships can be hard work, but don't take them for granted once you have received them. Some will be renewed automatically as long as you are continuously in school, but many will have to be applied for each year. In some cases, there may be strings attached to your scholarship or grant, such as maintaining a particular grade point average or continuing in a particular major or field of study.

There are a few basic questions you need to ask about each grant or scholarship you receive:

- Is the award renewable for each year that you are in college?
- What, specifically, do you have to do in order to maintain the award?
- Can the grant or scholarship be increased or decreased if your family's need changes?

If a grant or scholarship you receive is "one-time-only," be sure to factor that detail into your planning for later years.

Leadership Development Awards

Some financial aid awards focus on leadership development. Local groups, such as chambers of commerce, may have an interest in helping young people become leaders in the community. Some corporations enjoy the publicity that comes with helping to educate tomorrow's leaders, so be sure to avail yourself of any opportunities such companies may offer. Colleges often have scholarships designed to recruit or encourage student leaders.

Leadership awards are based on your local involvement in activities. Eligibility criteria vary but often include some demonstration of leadership in high school or your local community. Colleges tend to think of leadership broadly, so don't rule yourself out if you were not the president of an organization or the captain of a team. Leadership is about making a difference, and that is exactly what the college wants you to do upon coming to campus.

Alert

If you do receive an award from a company, community group, or other organization, it is appropriate to send each contributor a thank-you note. Your note can be brief, but be certain that it is sincere. Let the groups know that you appreciate their support and that their gifts will be put to good use.

Usually to win an award requires the completion of an essay or application, a personal interview, recommendations from teachers, an employer, or other adult mentor who knows you well.

ROTC

One of the best examples of leadership development aid is through the Reserve Officers' Training Corps (ROTC) program. Students who choose to pursue this route for scholarship aid often find generous assistance for their education costs. However, if you receive money from an ROTC program, you'll be obligated to complete some sort of military service upon graduation. Most ROTC programs want to train the best leaders for today's military branches, and if they invest in helping you become a leader, they will expect you to use that leadership to their benefit for a few years.

Work-Study Aid and Other Jobs

Work-study aid is money from federal, state, and/or college sources that is available to you if you work on campus. These jobs can pose a great opportunity because they are convenient and you can learn more about a particular department that interests you, form relationships with professors and other administrators, and earn money to fund your education.

 **Essential**

Even if you do not have a work-study award, try to find a job on campus. Working among staff and faculty is another great way to feel connected to your college.

Your campus probably has a work-study office, often located in the financial aid office or career center. Contact this office to find out how to secure a job on campus. Be sure to ask if your campus guarantees jobs for students with a work-study award. Here are some options for work-study jobs:

- ☐ If you have a special skill, such as lifeguard certification, you may be able to secure a desired job quickly
- ☐ College food service or maintenance programs always have jobs available
- ☐ Tutoring can often be a paid, on-campus position
- ☐ Apply to be a campus tour guide
- ☐ Be a campus ticket taker at entertainment events such as movies, plays, or visiting performances
- ☐ Look into getting a job at your school library, gym, cafe, admission, or administration offices

Check with career services, human resources, or in the student newspaper for other on-campus openings. Also, local business owners close to campus may also desire seasonal student help. Look for advertisements on campus, and again, check with your career services department. Also, check with your school to see if any off-campus jobs are eligible for work-study programs. This is not always possible, but some schools offer that as an option.

Loans

Educational loans are a component of almost every financial aid package. They represent borrowed money that you or your parents must repay, usually with interest. The Federal Stafford Loan and Federal Perkins Loan are common low-interest loans available to students who have demonstrated financial need. Before your loan funds can be credited to your account, you must complete an entrance interview to learn about your rights and responsibilities. Your school may offer a group interview, you may be able to do this one-on-one with a financial aid counselor, or you may be able to do this online.

Subsidized Loans

Subsidized loans are based on a student's calculated need. If there is a difference between the cost of your education and your scholarships, work-study award, and expected family contribution, then you will qualify for a subsidized loan. The government will pay the interest on the subsidized loans while you are in college or during grace periods. If the financial aid package your school offers you meets your demonstrated need, you will not qualify for subsidized loans.

Unsubsidized Loans

Unsubsidized loans are need-blind, meaning that they are available to students regardless of individual or family need in relation to the cost of the college. However, the interest is not deferred—it accrues while you are in school, and any unpaid interest rolls over and is added to your loan principal. Because of this, unsubsidized loans tend to be more expensive than need-based loans and should probably be used as sparingly as possible.

Loans for Parents and Families

Many loans are directed toward the student, but parents are often able to take on loans to help cover the difference between the cost of the education and the total financial aid offered. Parents may be able to borrow through a home equity loan or through the federal PLUS program. PLUS loans have a variable interest rate, and repayment of these loans must begin soon after the full loan amount is sent to the college. Families that take out loans to pay for a college education should check with a financial adviser or tax preparer to see if they qualify for a student loan interest deduction.

Questions to Ask

Students and families considering loans need to be careful about the balance between long-term debt and meeting education costs. Before you talk to a financial aid officer or other financial adviser, put together a list of questions about the loans you are considering. In addition to questions specific to your situation, be sure to ask:

- ☐ What are the terms of the loan?
- ☐ Is the loan subsidized or unsubsidized?
- ☐ How much will you owe by the time you graduate?
- ☐ What kind of monthly payments can be expected?
- ☐ What is the interest rate for the loan? Is it fixed or variable?

☐ Does the loan involve an up-front insurance payment or other additional fees?

☐ What is the maximum amount available from each lender?

☐ Are there any deferment or cancellation provisions associated with the loan?

It's very important for you to understand your complete financial aid package and how loans fit into the big picture. You want your loan debt to be manageable, so take advantage of every other opportunity, such as work-study or other employment, before relying on loans. When you do take on loans, do not borrow any more than you actually need.

Cost Versus Value

Students head to college to further their education and to have an opportunity for a better life. The cost of an education is significant, but the value of a college degree is proven to be even more significant. When you are considering colleges, look at more than just the price tag for your education. The prestige of an institution, for example, or the acclaim of a particular department there is an intangible aspect that can affect the perceived worth of your degree. Remember, also, that the value of an education goes well beyond your experiences in the classroom.

 **Essential**

Remember that you are not alone in your search for financial aid. Ask your parents to ask their bosses and colleagues about opportunities that are available. Your high school guidance counselor, coaches, and teachers may also have some good leads. If you worked during high school, ask your boss for help—particularly if you worked for a national chain store.

As you compare your final list of schools, look at each school very carefully. Ignore the prices for a moment and look at other indicators of value. These include:

- Qualifications and involvement of the faculty
- Class sizes and student-to-faculty ratio
- Specialized areas of study
- Opportunities to study beyond the campus
- Opportunities to use the latest technology
- Experimental education, such as study-abroad opportunities
- Social life on and around campus
- Continuing services for alumni
- Placement of alumni in leading graduate programs
- Demonstrated success of alumni in the workplace

You may find that the college you deem most valuable is more expensive than you had hoped, even if the school offers a generous financial aid package. In this case, you and your family must then weigh the immediate cost of loans against the total value of the education at that particular college. Looking only at cost will shortchange your opportunity for an exceptional education and college experience.

Likewise, judging less-expensive schools to be providers of less-valuable educational opportunities is unwise. Many community and state colleges, particularly if you take advantage of their honors programs, provide educations competitive with the offerings of many private schools for half the price. Do some research, talk to the experts, and make the decision that fits your needs and aspirations.

Financial Aid Tracker

Use the following list to keep track of financial aid information for your potential schools.

School: _____

Tuition and Fees: $_____

Room and Board: $_____

Other Expected Expenses: $_____

Financial Aid Forms:

☐ FAFSA

☐ Other: _____

Financial Aid Deadline: _____

Scholarships and Other Available Financial Aid:

Application Sent: _____

Notes:

_____

_____

School: _____

Tuition and Fees: $_____

Room and Board: $_____

Other Expected Expenses: $_____

Financial Aid Forms:

☐ FAFSA

☐ Other: _____

Financial Aid Deadline: _____

Scholarships and Other Available Financial Aid:

Application Sent: _____

Notes:

_____

_____

_____

School: _____

Tuition and Fees: $_____

Room and Board: $_____

Other Expected Expenses: $_____

Financial Aid Forms:

☐ FAFSA

☐ Other: _____

Financial Aid Deadline: _____

Scholarships and Other Available Financial Aid:

Application Sent: _____

Notes:

_____

_____

_____

School: _____

Tuition and Fees: $_____

Room and Board: $_____

Other Expected Expenses: $_____

Financial Aid Forms:

☐ FAFSA

☐ Other: _____

Financial Aid Deadline: _____

Scholarships and Other Available Financial Aid:

Application Sent: _____

Notes:

_____

_____

_____

School: _____

Tuition and Fees: $_____

Room and Board: $_____

Other Expected Expenses: $_____

Financial Aid Forms:

☐ FAFSA

☐ Other: _____

Financial Aid Deadline: _____

Scholarships and Other Available Financial Aid:

Application Sent: _____

Notes:

_____

_____

_____

School: _____

Tuition and Fees: $_____

Room and Board: $_____

Other Expected Expenses: $_____

Financial Aid Forms:

☐ FAFSA

☐ Other: _____

Financial Aid Deadline: _____

Scholarships and Other Available Financial Aid:

Application Sent: _____

Notes:

_____

_____

_____

School: _____

Tuition and Fees: $_____

Room and Board: $_____

Other Expected Expenses: $_____

Financial Aid Forms:

☐ FAFSA

☐ Other: _____

Financial Aid Deadline: _____

Scholarships and Other Available Financial Aid:

Application Sent: _____

Notes:

_____

_____

_____

CHAPTER 3

Preparations Before Heading to Campus

Once you have committed to a particular college, you'll be contacted by various college offices on a regular basis via e-mail, snail mail, and even by phone. You'll be congratulated, given surveys, and provided with key information to help you make a successful transition to college life. You may feel as if the college is still courting you, and in a way, it is. It wants to remind you that you made the right decision. However, much of the information is important and will help you get off to a good start at your new school.

Advice on Bills and Financial Materials

Few things are less exciting than a bill, and few things are more important. Remember the following when getting bills from your new college:

- Keep all financial papers you receive from your college in one place so that you can keep track of and review them as necessary.
- As each bill arrives, read it carefully. Make sure you understand which office is sending the bill, the amount due and due date, and the consequences for late or missed payments. Some billing information is very specific. At most colleges you *must* make an initial payment to hold your space in the class. You may also have to provide a deposit in order to guarantee housing.
- Note deadlines and penalty fees assigned to each bill. If you miss a particular payment, will you be charged interest on the amount due or assigned a fixed penalty amount?
- Keep a record of payments you submit. If there is any question about when or whether you made a payment, you should be able to immediately tell someone what you paid, when you paid it, and other details of the transaction.

When you receive a bill, here is what to do:

☐ Each bill includes a phone number to call if you have questions. Don't hesitate to call this number to get an explanation of the bill, how it fits into the big picture of the cost of college, and what payment options you have.

☐ Look closely at each bill you receive and make sure that you are only paying legitimate bills.

☐ Your college will probably only send you a single bill for all official expenses, such as tuition, fees, room, and board.

☐ Don't be afraid to ask questions. The person answering the phone has probably heard every imaginable question, so don't be shy or worry that your question is stupid. Do what it takes to help you understand this unfamiliar and complicated process. While keeping track of this information may seem tedious, it will make your life much easier if difficulties arise.

🔔 Alert

Look closely at each bill you receive and make sure that you are only paying legitimate bills. Private companies may send you bills for services or products that you do not need or want. Read everything carefully.

Health Insurance Basics

One of the earliest contacts you will receive will be from the college's health center. You may need to have a physical and provide proof that you have received various vaccinations. Look carefully at the due date for providing this information and make an appointment with your family physician accordingly. If you are unable to get to a doctor in time, call your college health center and see if they can provide the necessary services after your arrival on campus. Some items must be completed before you can begin classes or move into your residence hall, while others will be able to wait for a few weeks. Ask about flu vaccinations as well. Sometimes it is much less costly to get these on campus for a student fee as opposed to getting it administered by your doctor at home before you go.

HEALTH TO-DO LIST BEFORE YOU LEAVE

☐ Provide up-to-date immunization records showing vaccines including meningitis, MMR, varicella, and a TB screen. This is so important that the school may assess stiff penalties to you for noncompliance.

☐ Let your school's heath center know about any special medical needs or conditions you may have. For example, if you have diabetes or asthma, you need to let the professionals at the college know so they can further communicate how they can serve you.

☐ Find out which local pharmacies will fill your existing or any future prescriptions. See if they deliver, too! Sometimes that extra fee can be helpful when you are "stranded" on campus. Be sure your health insurance membership is registered at or linked to that pharmacy.

☐ Find out how to ensure that your personal physician can effectively communicate with the health center. You'll likely have to complete some additional forms to enable that communication. The important thing for you to learn is how the health center can help you meet your medical needs, either in their office or through community resources.

☐ Compare your school's health care plan with your own families' plan. Some colleges have health care plans for students and will send information about those plans to you early in the summer. Read through the costs and benefits carefully, comparing the school's package to what you may be eligible for with your family's insurance.

✅ Fact

Most colleges will be required by their state to have you provide up-to-date immunization records, including meningitis, MMR, varicella, and a TB screen. This is so important that they may assess stiff penalties to you for noncompliance. Knowing that this is probable, work with your parents to get the information together long before move-in weekend—maybe in the prior spring. Preplanning helps eliminate last-minute stress.

☐ If you will use your family's coverage at school, check for eligible health care providers that are near your school. Your family's insurance may not cover you at college, in which case some version of the school plan will be necessary. If your school does not offer a health care plan (which is increasingly the case at smaller schools, since the recent health care legislation made it possible for adult students to stay on their parents' plan longer), you can still search for health care coverage at *www.ehealthinsurance.com* for starters.

☐ Many schools will automatically assign you to their health insurance plan and require you to provide proof of alternate insurance if you want to opt out of their plan.

Safety and Your New Room or Apartment

Campus safety refers not only to when you are out and about but is also about protecting your belongings while they are at school. Consider the following in your planning for school:

☐ Look into insuring your belongings. Colleges do not carry insurance that covers theft or damage to student property. Unless the school is negligent, which rarely happens, you'll be responsible for repair and replacement costs of damaged or stolen items.

☐ If your family's homeowner's insurance does not cover your belongings while you're at college, you should consider signing up for renter's insurance, either through a school-sponsored program or an insurance agency.

☐ Record the serial numbers of all electronic equipment and make an estimate of the value of your books, clothing, and other belongings. Petty theft occurs on most college campuses, and occasionally a pipe leak, storm, or other problem will cause your belongings to be damaged.

☐ Consider investing in a small footlocker or lock box that you can keep hidden in your room with some of your valuables or important papers (for example your passport, cash, jewelry, etc., that you feel you need to have nearby in your room). Or check to see if your local bank will rent you a safety deposit box for items you feel you need to have at college but need to be kept fireproof or in a safer location than your dorm room or apartment.

☐ When you speak with an insurance agent, talk about replacement costs for your belongings.

Housing How-Tos

Sometime between April and early June, you'll receive materials about housing on campus. Pay close attention to the forms you receive and dates by which you must return those forms to the school. In some cases, late return of the forms will mean that you are placed on a waiting list or are not eligible at all for campus housing.

Complete the roommate questionnaire, which will be used to match you with a roommate, very thoughtfully and in great detail.

☐ Fill out these forms by yourself. Parents often want to fill them out with you or even complete them on your behalf, but it is important that this information represents you and your preferences.

☐ Be completely honest. If you smoke, say so—even if your parents don't know it. If you truly like classical music, mention this, even if you've been made fun of for it in the past.

☐ If there is some important fact or detail about yourself that is not asked for on the form and you want to share, by all means do it. Write anything extra that you think will assist the housing office in matching you up

Here are some questions to ask or answer for the housing office, even if they do not ask:

- Do you have any food allergies?
- Are you a morning or night person?
- Do you plan to use your room to socialize, sleep only or study exclusively?
- Do you need to have music playing when you study (on speakers as opposed to in your ears)?
- Do you snore? Make noise when you sleep? Sleep walk?
- Do you plan to have friends, relatives or significant others sleep over from time to time if policy allows?

Remember that the survey is a snapshot of you at this moment. By November, you probably will have changed some of your preferences because of your new life at college. The same will be true for your roommate. You will each start on similar footing and will change over the course of the semester. Be prepared to deal with these changes.

Essential

When you were considering various colleges, a student may have called you offering to answer any questions you have. You may also remember your student tour guide from your campus visit. Look up these students in your college's online directory and contact them for answers to your questions. They will probably be flattered that you remembered them and happy to help you out.

Should You Choose a Roommate?

Some schools will give you the opportunity to request a particular roommate. However, almost every housing professional you can ask will advise against selecting a friend as a roommate. Living with a friend is much different than hanging out with him. College may seem like a large and unfriendly place—intimidating to someone new. But rather than live with your friend, try to live near him. You will benefit more from having another room to visit, and the two of you may make twice as many friends by living apart. You will also be free to be yourself, even if that means being different than you were in high school.

Residence Halls and Learning Communities

If you are given the opportunity to request a particular residence hall, consider your choices carefully. Here are some

questions to consider on how to go about selecting a residence hall (if applicable):

- Consider the amenities of a hall. How new is the building?
  Does it have air conditioning or central heating?
- Where is the hall located in proximity to dining halls, classroom buildings, or the sports fields you frequent?
- Does the building have traditional rooms with shared bathrooms, or is it arranged in suites with bathrooms shared
  only by a handful of people?
- Is it a co-educational dorm, housing both men and women?
  Are men and women on the same floor or are halls divided
  by gender only?
- Does your new campus offer learning communities
  whereby students with similar academic interests or majors
  are housed on a floor or residence hall together? Does that
  idea appeal to you?
- If you choose a learning community, is there an expecta-
  tion to participate in extra work outside of class, including
  workshops, field trips, and discussion groups in your residence hall?

Students with Disabilities

If you have a documented disability and believe you will
require accommodations while at college, you should contact the Center for Students with Disabilities either before
you come to college or as soon as you arrive. Most colleges

strongly encourage making contact no later than the first two weeks of school.

If your disability requires a certain dorm or living arrangement, like having to be on the first floor or special proximity to a bathroom or kitchen area for medical reasons or otherwise, then certainly notify and reach out to housing in advance to try to get your special requests met before you arrive at campus. At that point it could be too late to make changes easily. You will need to provide documentation of your disability and will most likely need to meet with a disability specialist.

It is probably best to access the college's website to find out how to go about making an appointment and what the documentation requirements are. If you have questions about your rights as a student with a documented disability, you may contact the Office of Civil Rights (OCR) in the state where your college is located.

Orientation

Your first major event as a college student will be orientation. Most orientation programs try to accomplish three broad goals:

1. **Orient you to campus.** You will need to know where to find your classes, where the library and computer labs are, where to find and how to use the fitness center, etc.
2. **Introduce you to expectations of college life.** Academic expectations, conduct policies, and school traditions will be covered.

3. **Break the ice.** The orientation program will help you get to know your classmates and begin building friendships that may last the rest of your life.

Question

What if I am too shy to approach other people?
Even if you have trouble initiating conversations, you still need to be out and about, giving other people the chance to approach you. If you experience a lull in a conversation, ask the others about their residence halls, homes, or hobbies. People enjoy a chance to talk about themselves, and this will give you insight into their personalities.

The orientation office will begin sending you information about particular programs, dates, and costs sometime in the spring. Pay attention to the particular details and options involved with orientation. Consider the following questions:

- Is orientation held in the summer or just prior to the start of classes?
- Is there one orientation for everyone or specific sessions for specific individuals? When do you need to arrive and where will you be staying?

You need to approach much of orientation seriously. If you learn things at this time, such as how to use the library effectively, you will not have to relearn them later. Remember:

- Come to orientation prepared to have fun.
- Keep an open mind and be careful not to judge others quickly. Your classmates will be as nervous and excited as you are, and in the rush to impress everyone, it is easy to start forming cliques.
- It's easy to make mistakes, so forgive yourself and others quickly if that happens. Get to know as many people as possible and be friendly to everyone.

Pre-orientation Programs

Some colleges have a special or pre-orientation option for new students. These programs often involve outdoor experiences, such as hiking, bicycling, or taking advantage of natural resources close to campus. Other programs focus on community service projects. Often a small additional cost is associated with these programs, and sometimes scholarships or fee waivers are available for highly motivated but financially strapped students.

Consider these special orientation programs carefully. In addition to the value of the specific program, you are able to move into your residence hall early and get to know a small group of people before the entire class arrives. For many students, this is an excellent transition to college. Participation in a pre-orientation program could be the first step to becoming president of an outdoors club or a member of a service fraternity.

 **Essential**

Judge people gently and give new people a second or third chance to make a good impression. Remember that most new students are nervous and will try very hard to make friends. If people around you seem overzealous or say the wrong things, be patient with them. You may find yourself acting similarly soon enough.

Questions to Ask at Orientation

Make a list of all the questions you'd like to ask while you're at orientation:

CHAPTER 4

The Big Move

So, you're leaving home and beginning a new life. It's time to pack everything you own and prepare to move it, right? Wrong. You are moving from an apartment or house to a single room—a single room you will likely share with someone else. You're moving from your previously permanent home to a place where you will live for only nine or ten months out of the year. Keeping this in mind, you should only take what you will need, will really use, and can transport back and forth several times over the next few years.

Packing for a College Room

The first things you need to know are the size of your room and how many students will be sharing that space. Most students move into a residence hall room for their first semester of college, but if you are moving into a college suite or an apartment, you need to know how much space you have to yourself and how much you are sharing with others. Keep in mind that much of the floor space in your room will be filled by your bed, desk, and dresser. You have to think creatively and in three dimensions.

Here are some questions to ask or consider:

- What can be stacked in the room (such as crates or shelves)?
- What can hang from the back of the door (shoe racks, hooks, over-the-door mirrors)?
- What can be stuffed in the back of your closet or under your bed?
- Is there space for furniture, such as a futon or lounge chair?
- Will you need extra lighting, such as a desk lamp, clip-on light, or floor lamp?
- Will you be able to use items you purchase again the following year, even if you change rooms?

It's a good idea to hold off on purchasing some of these items until you have lived in your college room for a while. Most residence halls are equipped with the essential pieces of furniture. If you do accumulate an extra chair or bookshelf, consider where you will store the furniture during the summer and how you will transport it to storage depending on available transportation options

Here are some ideas for a prepacking checklist of things to do before move-in day:

- Try doing a dry run of packing your vehicle prior to moving to be sure you can get everything you need—including you and your parents—into the car. If it is too full, eliminate bulk items that can be purchased upon arrival such as pillows, blankets, or even food, cleaning, or hygiene items you planned to use to stock up in advance.
- Price and reserve a rental vehicle or U-Haul if your car will not hold your items.
- Consider packing in clear containers or zipper bags that can double as storage spaces when you get to your room. Clear stackable containers work very well under beds and lofts since you can see what is contained inside and they keep out dust.
- Be sure you have the proper packing supplies such as boxes, tape, markers to label, suitcases, crates, etc.
- Have your parents check with their insurance agent to see if you can get any "student away at school" discount while you are not living primarily at your home residence. For example, some policies allow that if a student lives more than 150 miles from home and only uses the family car on beaks, they can get a reduced premium.
- Confirm your flight reservations if you are flying to school and learn about your airlines' baggage restrictions and allowances.

- Reserve a hotel room for the night before and night of move-in for your parents and you and then just your parents once you are settled into your dorm or apartment.
- Find out the soonest date your school accepts boxes and packages to be sent to campus to assure your items will be accepted on campus prior to your arrival.

The key to packing for a residence hall room is to take only those things you will need from the time you move in until the next time you visit home. Avoid unnecessary duplication of items as well. For example, don't bring two pairs of sneakers unless you will need them for different activities. Buying food in bulk may seem cost effective, but large bags and boxes will quickly eat up the space in your car and your residence hall room. One case of bottled water may store well under your bed, but several cases may take up too much valuable storage area.

Essential

Small or rural towns may not have stores with specialty products that you rely upon. If your college is in such an area and you generally use a very specific hair or skin care product, for example, make sure you bring an extra supply with you. You can always stock up when you go home for a break, but you don't want to run out in the meantime. Also, do not forget about online ordering, which is often less expensive anyway. Amazon.com and Drugstore.com, for example, offer great deals on thousands of products.

You may decide to make a list of things that your family can mail to you if you find you really need them. And remember: If you will be moving from far away, you can purchase many things once you get to college, especially bulkier items like pillows, bedding, or towels, or more fragile items such as a computer printer or wall mirror.

Here are some more ideas for dorm essentials:

- School supplies you can bring from home: paperclips, highlighters, Post-its, pens, pencils, hole punch, stapler, tape roll, etc.
- Laundry supplies: Rolls of quarters, detergent, laundry bag, stain remover, dryer sheets, laundry basket
- Bathroom essentials: see list in the next section
- Seasonal clothing
- Dorm decorations, photos, personal items that make you feel at home (also many can be purchased at school). Special removable tape or putty to affix items to room walls. A bulletin board is also a good idea since many campuses do not allow nails or thumb tacks in walls.
- Supplemental lighting (desk lamp, floor lamp—can be purchased when you get to school since fragile)
- Fan to help with temperature issues
- Bedding, extra pillows, mattress pad, comforter, blanket, sheets, etc. to make you feel comfortable (Pillows take up lots of space, so consider purchasing those when you get to campus.)
- Small vacuum or dust buster as well as paper towels, baby wipes, or anti-bacterial wipes for spills

- Sleeping bag for guests
- Lanyard for your room keys and student ID
- Hangers, over-the-door wall hooks, and other closet organizers or over-the-door space savers for shoes, hats, coats, etc.
- Sewing and small first-aid kit
- A case of water or two upon arrival to store under your bed and to keep you hydrated.

Bathroom Essentials and Medications

Since you may be sharing a bathroom with everyone else on your floor, you need to be prepared to carry your toiletries to and from the bathroom each time you need to shower, brush your teeth, etc. The first thing you need is a bucket, basket, or some other kind of tote or shower caddy.

Your best bet is something plastic; it can withstand getting wet, and shampoo or other spills can be easily wiped off. You also want to get something that has openings on the sides or bottom to allow for water drainage. Finally, be sure to find something that is relatively small and has a handle. You only need to carry a few things for each trip to the shower, and something small will store unobtrusively in your room.

You may also want a small rug or bath mat for the shower and a shower caddy to take back and forth so you can dry off in your room if necessary. Or there may be a cubby or shelf in the common bathroom where you can leave your shower caddy.

There are a few toiletries and accessories you should bring with you to college, but remember that you can restock at your college's convenience store or your college town's local grocery store and pharmacy as needed:

- ☐ Soap and soap dish or body wash
- ☐ Toothbrush
- ☐ Toothbrush case
- ☐ Toothpaste, dental floss, and mouthwash
- ☐ Hairbrush or comb
- ☐ Hair dryer, if you use one
- ☐ Shampoo and conditioner
- ☐ Lotion (and sunscreen depending on location)
- ☐ Tissue (for use in your dorm room)
- ☐ Cotton swabs
- ☐ Nail clippers and file
- ☐ Shaving cream and razors
- ☐ Deodorant
- ☐ Contact lens care equipment, if needed
- ☐ Over-the-counter medication for allergies, headaches, joint pain, stomach distress

Since everyone on your floor will be using the same set of showers, you should get a pair of flip-flops or shower shoes. Some college bathrooms are cleaned regularly by custodial staff, but many students still feel more comfortable keeping something between their feet and the tile floor of the shower. If you purchase shower shoes, get something open and durable.

What *not* to bring to school:

- Hot plates
- Mini-refrigerators (unless allowed)
- Halogen lamps
- Candles
- Incense that requires you to light a match
- Weapons of any kind
- Posters or wall hangings with inappropriate messages

Check your dorm or apartment building for a specific restrictions list.

Technology items to bring to school (or purchase there if necessary):

- Laptop, desktop, or tablet
- Backup hard drive or zip drives
- Printer
- Extra ink cartridges
- Surge protector/power strips
- Extension cord
- Ethernet cable (if no WiFi access)
- Small, compact stereo or dock for your iPod or iPhone
- TV (if allowed)
- DVD player

⊕! Alert

Don't buy new clothes and immediately pack them for college. Wash them once and wear them a little bit to make sure they are comfortable before heading to school. Your well-planned wardrobe will do you no good if you get to campus and find that a garment doesn't fit or it shrinks the first time you wash it.

What to Wear

Your initial clothing selection should get you from move-in day to your first trip home. Consider the climate where your school is located and pack accordingly. If you go to college in the Northeast, you may want some sweaters, but you can probably leave the winter coat for your second trip. When you go home for fall break or Thanksgiving, you can take home summer and fall clothing and bring back winter items, such as coats, hats, scarves, and gloves. However, if your college is in the south, you may not need any winter clothing until second semester.

You may want to look your best all of the time, but you also need to be practical about how much space you have in your room. Here are some clothing questions to consider:

- How much dresser space will you have?
- Will you have a full closet to yourself, or will you have to share it with a roommate?

- How often will you have an occasion to wear that particular outfit? For example, is it something too formal for most college days?
- Will you be back home before a change of seasons to get your warm coat, rubber snow or rain boots, etc., or do you need those right away at your college?

You need to think about these things before you can make final decisions about what to bring with you.

Starting with the basics, you should plan to have about ten or twelve pair of underwear on hand. Though you will likely wash your clothes at least once a week, it's always a good idea to have some extras. This same rule of thumb applies to socks. There will be times, such as when you exercise, when you will change more than once in the same day.

You should also remember some additional clothing including:

- ☐ Bathing suit
- ☐ Bathrobe
- ☐ Exercise clothing
- ☐ Nice dress or sport coat and tie
- ☐ Pajamas
- ☐ Rain jacket and umbrella
- ☐ Sweaters
- ☐ Sweatshirts and sweatpants

Shoes

Shoes are an individual choice, but keep in mind that they take up a lot of space. You will definitely need at least one pair of each of the following: sneakers for exercise and athletics; flip-flops for the shower; dress shoes; and everyday shoes, such as loafers or walking sneakers. You may want hiking boots, if hiking is one of your interests, special shoes for biking, cleats for soccer or football, and other additional footwear. If sandals are your style, then you should absolutely bring a pair. Some students choose to have a pair of slippers for wearing around the residence hall.

Pajamas

It is necessary for you to bring pajamas or some other sort of nightwear. Residence halls are communal environments and you will need something appropriate to wear when you head to the bathroom in the middle of the night, or when you have to go outside for a fire drill at 4:00 A.M. You may choose to use T-shirts and sweatpants for sleeping, but make sure you plan for this when you pack. A bathrobe is a good idea too, particularly if it has pockets where you can keep your room key while you are in the shower.

Clothing Choices

Clothing is a personal statement about who you are and what makes you feel comfortable. On large campuses you may find a wide range of clothing types among the students. On smaller campuses, where many students might come from similar economic or geographic backgrounds, there may seem to be an unofficial uniform. When you visit campus, take note of what students are wearing; this may clue you in to the climate there, and give you an idea of just how "dressed up" people get for class. However, your clothing should express your personality and make you comfortable.

 **Essential**

Very few colleges have an official dress code for students. This being the case, many students feel comfortable wearing sweatpants, shorts, and even pajamas around campus and to class. Dining hall etiquette is similarly relaxed and many students wear baseball caps during meals. The rule of thumb for students on campus is comfort.

You will likely purchase a sweatshirt with your college's name or logo on it. You will have dozens of opportunities to purchase or win T-shirts. Some groups, such as athletic teams and Greek organizations, have their own casual wear, such as shorts, hats, and shirts.

Making It Feel Like Home

It is important to make your residence hall room feel a little bit like home. You will be sleeping, eating, studying, hanging out, and talking with family and friends on the phone all in this one room. You need to be comfortable here and make your guests feel comfortable as well.

Posters have long been a staple for college students. If you have some favorites, bring them along. If not, your college bookstore will sell them and poster vendors usually set up shop on campus during the first few weeks. Posters make a statement about you. Only display images you don't mind friends and family seeing.

Alert

Many colleges have restrictions on the use of wall hangings. Few schools allow you to hang things from your ceiling and none permit you to block smoke detectors and other safety equipment. Housing officials don't always allow nail holes in walls, and some kinds of tape will remove the paint or stain the wall. Make sure that you review your college's policies before affixing anything to your wall.

Many students bring photos of family, friends, and occasions, such as high school graduation. You will want a few framed photographs for your desk. You may be able to hang framed photos on your walls, but getting the frames to stick without damaging the wall may be difficult, depending on the construction of your building. Most students create a collage of photos around the desk or bed, adding to the collage as they take pictures of their college experiences. These collages can be a comfort to you and a great conversation starter with your new friends.

 **Essential**

Before your family leaves, make sure that you have everything you need. Once the car is unpacked, you can drive to local stores to pick up items that were too bulky to bring, such as a lamp or pillow. Once your family heads back home, you may not have the opportunity to run such errands for a while.

You will also want to bring some keepsakes, such as family photos, sentimental (but replaceable if lost or stolen) trinkets that remind you of home, artwork that you have created, etc., with you, but choose them carefully. The things you bring are likely to experience some wear and tear; they may be examined by visitors to your room, and, at worst, may be lost or stolen.

Other items that might be helpful to bring to school for fun and entertainment for you and your new friends are:

- Video games
- Board games
- Decks of cards
- Frisbee
- Football
- Soccer ball
- Tennis racket and balls
- Basketball
- Sketchbook and drawing supplies
- Magic 8 Ball

- Conversation starter games such as Table Topics
- Mad libs or other fun word games
- Journal

Start a list of the things you'd like to bring with you to college:

_____

_____

_____

_____

_____

_____

_____

_____

_____

_____

_____

_____

_____

_____

_____

_____

_____

_____

_____

_____

Moving Out and Summer Storage

Loading your belongings into a vehicle (or shipping them by post office or flying them by airplane) and heading to college for the first time will be exciting and fun. At some point, however, you are going to have to pack all of it up to get it home again. In the interim months you will have accumulated new books, clothing, and other items.

Sometime mid-semester, you should identify the items you are not going to use for the rest of the year and ship them home. If family or friends come to visit, send some things back with them. If you head home for spring break or take a weekend trip with your new friends to show them where you grew up, take some things home and leave them there.

Essential

Many students don't begin packing their rooms until exams are finished, and many parents are frustrated when they arrive and find a room that is completely unpacked. In addition to taking things home throughout the semester, use study breaks during finals week to pack items you don't need anymore. The more you have done before your family arrives, the better.

You may find that many of the things in your room won't be needed again until you return to college for your second year. Why take them home just to leave them in boxes? Inquire with your housing office about storage companies in the area around your college. Most schools cannot provide storage space but will know where students can rent a storage locker for the summer. To be most cost-effective, rent a locker with several friends, splitting the cost and adding help with moving heavy items.

CHAPTER 5

Roommates and Dorms

Your roommate may be the person who wakes you up when you sleep through your alarm, who takes messages for you, and who brings you soup when you are sick. She may get you invited to great parties and get you involved in clubs or sports. Your roommate might lend you her favorite clothes, swap jewelry with you, and keep you up laughing for half the night. Or your roommate might simply be the person you share a room with for a few months. In any case, this person will be an important figure in your life.

Roommate Selection

Some colleges will give you a choice between picking your own roommate and being matched with another person. You may feel a greater sense of control if you pick your own roommate—either someone you know from high school or a new friend met during a campus visit or orientation. As long as each of you requests the other, your school will probably place you in the same room.

However, choosing your own roommate can backfire since living with someone is entirely different than just being his friend. Sometimes, the better you know a person, the more difficult it may be to manage the conflicts that arise. You need to have a long conversation with a potential roommate about how you're going to manage your room and your friendship. Ask one another:

- Can you resolve disagreements without dragging mutual friends into the conflict?
- What if your shared interests begin to diverge and you start to head in different directions?
- Because you're already friends, how much time do you expect to spend with each other while at college?

Even if you and a friend plan to attend the same college, there are benefits to deciding to live apart. If your friend lives elsewhere on campus, you will have another place to visit, you can double the number of people you meet, and it will likely be easier to preserve your valued friendship. After a semester of college, once you know what living with a roommate is all about, if you and your friend still want to try living together, it is probably worth a shot the next year.

Meet Your Roommate

If the school assigns you a roommate, keep in mind that you were likely paired intentionally—the housing staff probably hoped that you could learn from one another. Your roommate survey details your interests and preferences in several categories. Residential staff uses this information to match you with likely compatible roommates.

Once you know who your roommate will be, you should get in touch with him soon after receiving his contact information from your school. Most schools will send you your roommate's name, e-mail address, and phone number. Your initial contact with your new roommate, by whatever means, should be fairly generic. You could also look up the roommate you are assigned on social networking sites like Facebook to learn about him, if you receive the name in advance. It's a good way to get a peek into his life and interests before you room together.

Fact

Try not to make snap judgments about your new roommate based on her social network information. People put up a lot of information in jest or that is specifically targeted to their friends that might lead you to the wrong conclusion.

You want to get to know this person and let him get to know you, but neither of you wants to overwhelm the other. Here are some questions you could ask during your first conversation:

- Why did you choose this college?
- How many brothers and sisters do you have? Are they older or younger than you?
- How are you spending your summer?
- Do you have a major yet?
- Are you involved in sports, theater, band, or other activities?
- Do you have pets?
- When can you talk again?

In your next conversation you want to get to know him a little better and begin to plan for move-in day. You probably want to wait to ask about preferences such as having guests in the room or how loud to play music, unless these things are deeply important to you. Questions you could ask during the second conversation include:

Alert

Though a rare occurrence, it's possible that even after you've begun getting to know your roommate over the phone or through e-mail, he will make the decision not to attend your college after all. If this happens, contact your housing office as soon as possible. You'll be matched with a new roommate quickly so you can adapt to this change before move-in day.

- What do you like to do for fun?
- How would you like to decorate the dorm room?
- Which appliances or decorations can you bring on move-in day? (Some students find it useful to keep a running list on a notepad, their phone, an e-mail or shared document with a list of items each will bring, adding to it as you remember, buy, or acquire them.)
- Do you know anybody else who will be attending the college?
- What classes are you planning to take?

Between phone conversations you should use the social networking strategy best suited to the two of you to stay in touch with your new roommate. You don't want to appear too eager, but you do want to continue to get to know this person better. Prior to arriving on campus, you should have at least one more phone conversation with your roommate. This final conversation can cover more personal territory and include some of the following questions:

- Are you in a relationship? If so, will your significant other be visiting the room often?
- What kind of social life are you hoping to find at college?
- What is your favorite movie, book, or song, and why?
- What will you miss most about your family?
- Are you a morning or a night person?
- Are you a light or heavy sleeper?
- Do you need total quiet when studying or can someone be on the phone or playing music while you study?

- How do you feel about sharing clothing or borrowing items from one another?
- Are you a smoker or drinker?
- How often do you like to clean?
- If there are costs or bills relating to your living together, how would you plan to split them?
- What are you most looking forward to about college?

If you lay the groundwork for a friendship with your roommate, you will increase your chances for a successful living arrangement. And by discussing important matters before you even arrive at school, you can avoid messy arguments and set the tone for open roommate communication.

Essential

Most students come to college believing that conflict should be avoided. This unrealistic impression can make roommate relations very difficult. Be prepared to disagree with your roommate and plan to work through your differences. Honest, private conversations will solve most of your problems, and your RA will help with the rest.

If there are more issues you'd like to discuss with your new roommate, list them here:

_____

_____

_____

_____

Lasting Relationships

Your roommate will definitely be a big part of your college life, but she might also become a bridesmaid in your wedding, a godparent to your child, or a lifelong travel partner. These meaningful relationships don't occur just because you and your roommate listed similar preferences on a survey, or because you had a lot of fun living together for a semester. The roommate relationship, like any other, requires reciprocal attention to survive. Your roommate could end up being a friend for life if you nurture the friendship for years and recognize that you both were sharing your lives in an intimate and special way through an important stage in your life.

Here are some tips on starting off right with your new roommate:

- Focus on finding things that you have in common and build on those. Even if you dress differently or enjoy opposing forms of entertainment, perhaps you both appreciate the same foods or have similar study habits.
- Manage your initial expectations. Be realistic about your new roommate. This person is probably just as excited, nervous, and inexperienced as you are regarding college, roommates, and future plans.
- When you first start living together, most initial conflicts and annoyances will be glossed over. Neither of you will want to make a bad impression or be a bad roommate. Taking this into account, be patient with yourself and your roommate as you get to know each other those first few weeks.

- Be prepared to disagree with your roommate and plan to work through your differences. Honest, private conversations will solve most of your problems, and your RA (Residence Assistant) will help with the rest.
- Don't be too hasty in your judgment of your roommate. For example, if you learn that your roommate likes classical music, you may picture an antisocial geek with no sense of humor. Be patient with yourself and your roommate, and be prepared to change your opinion several times throughout your roommate relationship.

Moving In

When you actually get on campus and move into your room, you need to do a few things before unpacking:

☐ Pay careful attention to directions provided in your orientation materials. When arriving on campus for move-in day, you may have to report to a particular area first. Also, since hundreds of other students will be moving in at the same time, your campus is likely to have particular directions for unloading your belongings and parking the family car.

☐ Inspect the room. Try the phone, test the desk and dresser drawers, open windows and closets, check both sides of your mattress for tears, and search the walls for damage. Report any concerns to your RA or ask for a room condition form to note any repairs that need to be made or damage that exists before you unpack. Keep your list so that you are not held accountable for the damage when you move out of your room at the end of the school year.

☐ As you and your family unpack your belongings, don't worry too much about getting things set up just right. You and your roommate will likely rearrange the room at least once in the first month of school. You do want to get clothes put away, hang a few things on the walls, and store suitcases or boxes that you are not sending back with your family.

☐ If you have a refrigerator, make sure it is located near an outlet and plugged in.

☐ Place electronics near the appropriate outlets. If you bring a TV, it must be near the cable outlet and your computer near the network connection if the hall is not wireless.

☐ Connect your computer and make sure that nothing was damaged during the trip to campus. If you're having difficulty connecting to the campus network, talk to your RA about how to get help.

After you've mostly set up your room, walk around the building and get the lay of the land. Learn where the lounges are, if there's a kitchen in the building, and where laundry and vending services are located. If you still have time before orientation activities begin, take a quick tour of the campus with your roommate. This will give you a sense of where your residence hall is in relation to classes, the cafeteria, the library, and other places you will visit often in your new life.

Roommate Agreements

During your first few weeks of college, you and your roommate may get along perfectly. But before long, academic stresses, conflicting schedules, boyfriends and girlfriends, or a lack of space may begin to complicate things. The best time to start working on conflict is before the conflict actually occurs, and this proactive approach can begin with a roommate agreement.

Essential

Initially, roommates tend to be too general when negotiating agreements. For example, each will agree to "respect" the other without defining that term. In fact, such concepts can have very different meanings, depending on where a person grew up and how she was raised. Be as specific as possible when discussing each item in your agreement.

Your RA may approach everyone on the floor about completing and posting formal roommate agreements. If this is the case, begin with the form your RA provides. If your RA does not provide a form, sit down with your roommate and write down a few issues that are important to each of you. Some of these items may include:

☐ Sharing music, DVDs, books, and electronics
☐ Sharing clothing
☐ Sharing food
☐ Using items that are off-limits
☐ Using each other's computers
☐ Taking phone messages

After you have come to a consensus about these smaller points, you need to address more personal issues; these include things like privacy, sleep schedules, and visitor guidelines. These points will be harder to negotiate because they affect each of you more personally. Be honest about your desires and listen carefully to your roommate's views. If you are unable to come to agreement on an issue, ask your RA for guidance.

🅰️ Alert

People deal with conflict in very different ways. Some get angry, shout, and then forget about it. Others keep quiet and address the issue only after significant thought. Find out how your roommate deals with conflict, and then explain your own approach. Keep these different styles in mind as you work through your differences.

Use the following form to create a draft of your roommate agreement.

Date: _____

_____ and

_____ agree to the following:

_____

_____

_____

_____

_____

_____

_____

_____

_____

_____

_____

_____

_____

_____

_____

_____

_____

_____

Signed:

_____

_____

Your initial roommate agreement will get you through the first round of conflicts, and each of you will likely point out a violation of the agreement. As the semester wears on, you and your roommate will begin to change, and something you hadn't covered will inevitably become an issue. For example, if your roommate begins dating someone a few months into the school year, you may feel that this person's visits are infringing upon your privacy. If you didn't address the issue of significant others in your initial agreement, you will likely need to make an amendment at this time.

Managing Conflicts

No matter how well you get to know your roommate before arriving on campus or how well you design a roommate agreement, some kind of conflict will undoubtedly arise. This may be something trivial that simply annoys you or something much more serious. Whether the conflict occurred because someone put an empty milk carton back in the fridge or one roommate "stole" the other's iPod, every issue needs to be resolved.

If the conflict is minor, sit down with your roommate as soon as possible and discuss the issue—talk about why you are concerned and listen to what she has to say. After you have each had a chance to speak, work together to find a solution. If your conflict is more heated, you might be best served by stepping away for a while and calming down. Take a walk, call your family to vent (and explain that you are only venting, not asking for solutions), or go work out at the gym.

Once you have calmed down, approach your roommate about the situation. Again, explain your views and why the situation upset you so much, and then give your roommate a chance to respond. If she becomes upset, ask if she wants to take a break before discussing the situation further. But don't let things fester for long before you continue your conversation and work on a resolution.

Your college will also provide you with a great resource for working through roommate conflicts: your RA. This student has lived through what you are experiencing and has taken the RA job in order to help others. All RAs receive formal and informal training about roommate conflicts. So, when you are having difficulty with your roommate, knock on your RA's door and ask for some time to talk privately. Be completely open with your RA—she will keep your problem confidential.

Room Changes

On rare occasions, roommates will come to have irreconcilable differences. If this occurs, you will need to communicate the problem to your RA, your hall director, and perhaps someone else from your housing office. If everyone agrees that the situation cannot be remedied, the only solution is to separate you.

 **Question**

Which roommate moves when a conflict is irreconcilable?
If the roommates cannot agree, then the housing office will make the decision. The outcome will have nothing to do with money, grades, or personal connections to college staff. Many times the housing office will decide that the only fair thing is to move both roommates.

The decision to separate two roommates comes with complications. First, roommates will likely have to agree on a new living situation. If neither roommate has a replacement living situation in mind, the housing office will have to move one or both students out of the room. This change may discourage some students—they may fear their new roommate situations will be just as bad as, or worse than, the first. Additionally, neither roommate will likely want to leave his present floor or residence hall. However, due to a shortage of available space, at least one roommate might have to leave the place he has come to call home.

It is often harder for new students to change rooms in the fall semester. Residence halls are generally filled to capacity at this time, and there may be a waiting list for open rooms. If you're aware of a housing shortage on your campus, you need to be proactive and present your hall director or housing office with a solution. If you and your roommate can find another pair of roommates that wants to split, you can propose a simple swap. In this case, everyone involved must agree about who will be moving into which room. This can be a great solution, but it will require you and your roommate to work together until a consenting pair is found.

CHAPTER 6

Personal Finance at College

You've been told that being an independent adult comes with responsibility. One of the first big responsibilities you are about to assume is primary responsibility for your personal finances. You will have to make significant decisions that will affect your day-to-day life, as well as your future. When developing a budget, you will quickly learn what works for you and what does not.

Cash, School Charge Card, Check, Debit, or Credit

Although your basic needs are taken care of and you brought a lot of personal items from home, you'll eventually find yourself needing money for some extra purchases. You will buy essentials such as books, lab supplies, and pens. You'll also go out to eat, see or rent movies, and attend concerts. The key to balancing these expenditures is knowing how much money you have at all times, sticking to a budget, and choosing the best method of payment.

Cash

Cash in small amounts is one of the most popular means of payment on and around a college campus. You don't want to carry around hundreds of dollars or leave that much money hidden in your residence hall room, but you want to be able to purchase a cup of coffee on the way to class or go off campus for lunch with classmates. The big advantage to cash is that it is accepted everywhere and doesn't cost you anything in terms of interest fees or finance charges.

School Charge Card

Some colleges allow you to charge things internally, placing the charge directly on your bill or student ID card. With this option you don't have to part with any of your pocket cash or add a charge to your credit card, but your parents will likely see the bill and wonder just what they are paying for. If you use this method at all, do so with caution.

Checks

Checks are a popular means for making more expensive purchases. You will not have enough cash on hand to purchase all of your books for the semester, and your campus bookstore is likely willing to accept a personal check. Off-campus, you may have trouble using checks to pay for items, and if you write too many checks you may incur extra fees through your bank. But if you are going to write checks for purchases, be prepared to show a driver's license or other form of identification.

Debit Cards

Many students use debit cards to purchase anything from books to items from the convenience store. Debit cards are used like credit cards, but the money is transferred immediately from your bank account. These cards can be a better alternative to credit cards, since you aren't spending more money than you have in the bank. Keep a close eye on your balances, though—overdraft fees can be costly.

Credit Cards

Credit cards have the advantage of being accepted almost everywhere, including Internet shopping sites. Credit cards are more complicated than debit cards, cash, or checks, and warrant some extended discussion.

Should You Get a Credit Card?

Even though most colleges now prohibit credit card solicitation, advertisements may be stuffed in your bookstore bags, companies may send solicitations to your campus mailbox, and fliers may be posted around campus. There are good reasons to have a credit card, namely for emergencies, for travel, and to keep from carrying large amounts of cash. However, there are a number of pitfalls as well. Here are some things to think about before you sign up for one:

- The federal government enacted the Card Act of 2009, which, among other provisions, now required that people under the age of twenty-one have a co-signer (who is at least twenty-one years old), or provide proof of a way to repay before being issued a credit card. A good overview with more details can be found at: *http://en.wikipedia.org/wiki/Credit_CARD_Act_of_2009*
- Some credit card companies will give you something free just for signing up for their card. Be wary of such offers. If they are willing to give you something for free, what's in it for them?
- Compare credit card offers carefully and read all of the fine print before making a decision. A zero percent annual percentage rate (APR) looks great, but usually only last for a limited time. The lower your fixed APR, the better it is for your budget.
- Look at annual fees. Many cards charge you for the privilege of using their services.

- Most credit cards allow you to make charges or get cash advances, which are usually subject to a transaction fee and usually a higher interest rate. Your cash advance limit is often lower than your total credit limit.
- Use your credit card sparingly and for *charges only.*
- Plan on getting only one card, and find one with a low credit limit. You won't need more than a $1,000 limit even in emergencies, so anything more than that may affect your ability to make timely payments.
- Try not to carry your card with you at all times. If you don't carry the card regularly, you will be less likely to make impulsive purchases.

🔔 Alert

Some credit card companies will give you something free just for signing up for their card. You may receive a free item on the spot, they may mail you something once your application is approved, or they may "forgive" your membership fee. Be wary of such offers. If they are willing to give you something for free, what's in it for them? Read the fine print to be sure.

Remember that charging something actually increases its cost if you don't pay your credit card bill immediately. Missing payments or carrying a large balance can also hurt your credit rating. A damaged rating takes time to repair, and when you graduate you may find that you need a good credit rating to get yourself established in the next phase of your life.

Credit Reports

Any time you borrow money or use credit, your credit rating is affected. The following things are listed on your credit report:

- Apartment rent
- Student loans in the student's name
- Utilities under your name
- Bank loans
- Credit cards

When you try to get new credit, such as securing a new credit card or getting a loan to purchase a car or house, the lender you are working with will check your credit rating. If you have consistently paid your bills on time, you will probably get the credit you are seeking and get lower interest rates. However, the more problems you have on your report, such as missed payments or high balances, the more difficulty you will have getting credit.

🚨 Alert

Most credit cards allow you to make charges or get cash advances, and the latter deserve particular caution. Cash advances are usually subject to a transaction fee and sometimes a higher interest rate. Also, your cash advance limit is often lower than your total credit limit. Use your credit card sparingly and for charges only, if possible.

This all serves as a caution to you. You want to get through college with as little debt as possible. When you do incur debt, you want to treat it carefully. It's not only your college education that could affect you for years to come. If you start to be concerned about your credit rating, you should seek assistance quickly. There are nonprofit agencies that can help you understand your credit report and give you a crash course in personal finances (financial management) at no cost. Your local bank or college bursar's office may have resources that you can use, and your parents are a good source of counsel as well. These are better options than those that charge fees for the same services.

Finally, to obtain a free credit report annually, try: *www .annualcreditreport.com/cra/index.jsp*. For credit scores whenever you are curious, try *www.creditkarma.com* and *www .creditsesame.com*.

Finding a Local Bank

Many students and their families decide that the student should have an account with a bank in the town where the college is located. However, this may not be necessary. If you rarely use a bank at home, you may not use a bank often while at college, either. Perhaps the college has a check-cashing service or a safe to hold large sums of cash. You can certainly use those services and survive well at college, but check with your campus first to learn just what services they provide, as well as the limitations of those services.

Here are the advantages to having a local bank:

- Access to a full range of banking services and the ability to meet with bank staff when needed
- More control of your financial health, and it can be an excellent educational tool
- ATMs linked to your bank don't have additional cash withdrawal fees associated with them

Your experience finding a bank will vary depending on whether you are in a big city or a small town. The larger the town, the more banks that will be available. You may find that your home bank has a branch near your college through which you can access your existing account. You may also find that your college conducts business with a particular bank and has arrangements to help students bank there. Both cases can make your life a little easier.

When selecting a bank, understand the various account packages offered and how they fit with your banking needs. For example, you are unlikely to need unlimited checking if most of your spending will be done with cash or credit. Here are a few questions to ask before opening an account:

- ☐ What is the interest rate for each account?
- ☐ Is there a charge for writing checks?
- ☐ Do you have to maintain a minimum balance on each account? If so, what is the fee for not meeting it?
- ☐ What is the charge for bouncing a check?

☐ Can you link checking and savings accounts for over-draft protection?

☐ How often will you receive statements?

☐ Is there an extra charge for getting or using a bank (ATM) card?

☐ Where are other branches of the bank?

☐ Where are the bank's ATMs located?

ATMs

Keep a few warnings in mind when using ATMs. If your bank or network does not own the ATM you are using, there might be an extra charge for using that machine. Charges usually range from $0.50 to $2.00 per transaction. Frequent use of such ATMs will quickly deplete your bank account. Find an ATM that's in your network instead of regularly using machines that charge the extra fee. If you do use a machine that charges a transaction fee, be certain that you include that fee when you balance your checkbook.

Another option to consider is opening an account with a bank that reimburses all ATM fees, regardless of where you use their card nationwide. Try Allybank.com. Or, conduct a Google search for "banks that reimburse for ATM fees" for current listings near you.

• Be aware of your personal security when using an ATM. While most ATMs are in well-lit areas and are monitored by video surveillance, you still need to exercise caution at these machines. Shield the keypad when you enter your

PIN code so that nobody can read it over your shoulder. Also, take care to shield your PIN-typing from security cameras as well, since crooks have recently been caught installing their own tiny cameras at ATMs to record users entering their PINs and then robbing the cardholder. Be aware of who is around you while you are at the ATM, and don't count your money out in the open.

- Don't let yourself get distracted by anyone behind you in line or asking you a question while you are using the ATM. Many scam artists or crooks hang out near ATMs looking for unassuming victims. Don't be one who succumbs to distraction tactics.

Balancing Your Checkbook

Balancing your checkbook may be one of the most unexciting chores you will ever undertake. It is also one of the easiest things you can do to keep your financial life in order and prevent problems from surprising you. Balancing your checkbook is actually more than just keeping track of what check you wrote, when, and for how much. You need to give attention to how you are spending money, in all respects.

The good news is that there are as many methods of balancing your checkbook as there are people who spend money. A quick Internet search will turn up a variety of software products that will balance your checkbook, keep track of interest payments and due dates, and give you advice for managing your money. Some of these programs also work with tax software for people who file their own taxes. You can pick any of these products or keep a simple handwritten log of your accounts and spending.

ⓔ✺ Essential

Make sure to check your records against the statement provided by your bank. If there is a discrepancy between the two, call your bank right away and find out where the problem is. You may have forgotten to record a check or an ATM withdrawal, but it also may be that someone is using your bankcard without your knowledge. The same goes for credit cards.

Here are a few ideas on keeping your money safe:

- Never give out your password or PIN number to anyone, not even your roommate or close friends.
- Don't keep too much cash in your wallet or room, just as much as you need to hold you over. Use a debit or credit card when you can; if your wallet is lost or stolen you can at least cancel or freeze those cards. Once your cash is gone, it's gone.
- Hide your wallet in a "secret" not obvious pocket in your backpack, not an outside or easy access pocket for possible snoopers or thieves.
- Keep photocopies of your card numbers somewhere else outside of your wallet with contact phone numbers in case your wallet is misplaced or stolen.

- Keep government ID or a passport with your wallet only when you travel. Other than travel, your student ID often will work as supplemental ID should you need it.

Living on a Budget

You don't have to be an economics major to understand that your spending cannot outpace your income. Now that you are in charge of providing everything beyond your basic necessities, you need to establish a budget and stick to it. Parents are a good resource when you begin thinking about budgeting. Not only are they already familiar with your finances, they have managed a larger and more complex budget for an extended time.

You probably don't need a detailed budget for college life. Instead, think of general categories of spending and set an amount for each. After you have listed each category, total the amount you anticipate spending and compare that with your income and savings. If you're spending more than you're making, you need to find places where you can spend less. Some categories you should consider for your budget are:

Travel to and from home _____

Travel around town _____

Car maintenance and gasoline _____

Eating out and food deliveries _____

Entertainment, such as movies and concerts _____

Clothing purchases _____

DVD/CD/music and movie download purchases _____
Phone bills _____
Holiday and birthday gifts _____
Laundry _____
Toiletries and medications _____

Once you get to college, keep track of where your money is going. For example, if you take money from an ATM, record what you used it for. This will help you make adjustments to your budget when necessary. You should also build in some cushion for emergencies or spontaneous moments. Or, spend a month or so tracking your spending in the previous areas. Then, review by looking at the results and see where costs can be cut. For example, if you are spending way too much on food deliveries, you should think about picking up your food instead or cooking for yourself more.

Here are ways to save money on a daily basis:

- Look for special discounts available to college students. Many stores, restaurants, movie theaters, and auto shops near your college will likely offer student discounts. You'll simply need to present your student ID when you make your purchase.
- Some restaurants and shops offer coupons or stamp cards you can collect so that each time you go there you accumulate credit toward a free menu item or service.
- Find local happy hours or times of day that places offer a discount on food or beverages to anyone.

Following are some more detailed tips you can use to help limit your spending:

ENTERTAINMENT

- Share movies and games with trusted friends to add variety to your own collection.
- Seek out movies and music from your school's collection.
- Get a library card to your local community library.
- Use Hulu, Redbox, Netflix, or other entertainment database sources.

CELL PHONE

- Consider a prepaid plan or lower-cost unlimited plan that includes long distance, unlimited texts, data usage, and minutes.
- Use Skype or Google voice to supplement phone minutes and ensure that you stay within your budgeted minutes if you are not using an unlimited plan.
- See if your phone plan can be bundled into a family, group, or corporate plan with your parents to save some money.

SHOPPING

- Comparison shop online before buying, especially more costly staples such as printer ink cartridges.

- Recycle ink cartridges at your local office supply store; many offer cash back or store credit for future purchases.
- Extreme coupon! Go online to sites and stores that you frequent and look for deals. Stock up and buy in bulk on non-perishable items.
- Seek out thrift shops, bargain stores, garage sales, etc. for clothing.
- Use *www.groupon.com* or *www.livingsocial.com* (but be careful to only buy things you will need or actually use).
- Trim your own hair or bangs between cuts or find a friend who is good at it!

 **Essential**

Many residence hall rooms do not have air conditioning, but most campuses do not allow students to bring their own window air conditioning units. If you require air conditioning for health reasons, get in touch with your campus health services office as soon as possible. Otherwise, consider a window fan or an oscillating fan that you can move around the room.

TEXTBOOKS

- Rent books instead of buying.
- Sell books you are unlikely to use again.
- Rent books to other students you know who are also on tight budgets.

TRANSPORTATION

- Forgo bringing a car to campus until you are certain that you really need one. You will save on a parking permit, insurance, maintenance, registration, gas, and tickets for sure!
- Use public transportation where available. Walk and bike as much as possible. It is good for your health, too!
- Share rides home or chip in for gas if you are driving distance to get home for school vacations.

Finally, be prepared to say "no" to some activities. You simply can't go out to eat every night, go to every concert, or do other things that drain your budget. Finding no-cost entertainment won't be hard once you decide not to spend more money.

CHAPTER 7

Keeping Clean

You will quickly find that living in a residence hall room is vastly different than living at home. Your bedroom will now be your living room, dining room, kitchen, study, and late-night hangout. Because so much will be going on here, you and your roommate must decide not only how to arrange your furniture but also how to maximize and maintain the limited space you share.

Keeping a Clean Room

You and your roommate must agree upon how neat or messy to keep your room. If one of you is a slob and the other a neat freak, you are bound to get on each other's nerves from time to time. To manage such differences, it will help if you set some ground rules.

- ☐ Agree to dispose of pizza boxes and take-out food containers within twenty-four hours. You don't have to empty your trash every day, but perishable food will begin to smell if left in the garbage for too long.
- ☐ Plastic storage boxes under your bed are a great way to keep things organized and protected, as well as to move items to and from college.
- ☐ A plastic tray or cup will help you keep pens in one place.
- ☐ A small bottle or bucket will keep loose change and laundry money available for use.
- ☐ Hooks on the back of the door are an ideal way to store bathrobes and jackets.

Keep in mind that friends are more likely to hang out in your room if it is relatively clean and there are places for them to sit. You can leave study materials out on your desk and a sweatshirt draped on the back of your chair, but if you have piles of dirty clothing on the floor, people will not feel comfortable in your room.

There are a few specific items that you should have in your room to keep it looking and smelling clean.

- A can of air freshener or odor eliminator, such as Febreze. This can help you mask or eliminate the odor of take-out food that may remain after you've eaten it, or you can spray it into your garbage can every time you change the bag.
- A spray bottle of glass cleaner or all-purpose cleaner and paper towels will also be helpful. If you spill juice on the floor, this will get rid of any stickiness, and you can also use these products to dust the surfaces of your desk, dresser, and mirror.
- Cleaning wipes or antibacterial wipes are invaluable for small spills, dusty surfaces, shelves and windowsills, or even dirty hands.
- A broom and dustpan or small vacuum are also helpful as well as a small bucket or crate in which to store cleaning supplies.
- Hand sanitizer, a large pump for your desk.
- Special spray for your computer screen or other electronic devices. Check with your school's technology help desk for information on cleaning and protecting these items.

Also, remember not just to clean your room, but make a checklist list to remind yourself to:

☐ Throw out unused or spoiled food from your refrigerator each week
☐ Vacuum and dust once a week
☐ Do your laundry every week so it doesn't smell
☐ Wash your dishes after you use them

Laundry Lessons 101

It turns out that doing laundry is just a little more complicated than throwing clothes in the washer, adding some detergent, and coming back later to put everything in the dryer. Or rather, it is a little more complicated if you want your clothes to look good and last for a while. In order to keep your clothes in good shape, you'll need to work out a laundry schedule, learn to sort your clothes according to material and color, and organize a laundry budget.

Laundry Basics

Figure out how often you need to do laundry—once a week is usually sufficient. Don't wait until you're wearing your last pair of clean underwear to drag a heaping basket to your residence hall laundry room.

 Essential

If you borrow clothing from a friend, it is appropriate to wash the clothing before returning it. Items such as sweaters and outerwear may not need to be washed unless they have acquired a stain or smell of smoke. If you cause damage that cannot be easily repaired, you should replace the garment.

Keep in mind that everyone else in your residence hall will have to do laundry as well, and there will probably only be one machine for every thirty students. Weekend afternoons and Sunday nights are typically peak laundry times in residence halls, so consider choosing another time to avoid the crowds. If you can stick to a consistent laundry schedule, you will be better able to manage your time and will always have something clean to wear.

Here are some laundry tips:

☐ Have rolls of quarters on hand if the machines are coin-operated. If your laundry room machines use card readers, make sure you have enough money loaded on the card to do a few loads of laundry.

☐ Make sure you have detergent and dryer sheets on hand.

☐ Sort clothing into groups by color and material. Read the tags on your clothing to see if any items warrant special care; if so, place those items in a separate pile. At the very least, separate light and dark colors.

☐ Whenever possible, separate delicates from heavier items.

☐ Check all your pockets, remove pins or stickers you placed on your clothing, and tie drawstring ends together. Tying up drawstring ends (on a hooded sweatshirt, for example) will keep the string in place throughout the washing and drying process.

☐ Be sure that each pile of laundry is the right size. Too few items will waste water in the washing cycle, and too many items can overload the washer and keep the dryer from being effective.

☐ Choose a general-purpose detergent. Determine if you like powder, liquid, or the newer pods/packets better and what your machine prefers as well.

☐ Be sure to check your laundry toward the end of the cycle to be sure you are the one changing your clothes from the washer to the dryer. Some students help themselves to washing machines when the cycle ends and heap your clothes somewhere without your consideration.

☐ Some students put a sticky note on the machine with their name, room number, cell number and the time so that the next person using the machine will hopefully notify them in the event that they might forget about their clothes. Pay it forward.

☐ The correct water temperature depends on what type of clothing you are washing. Many clothing labels will list what temperature the water should be, and college laundry rooms often have temperature guides posted on the walls to assist you. Use cold water for dark colors and new clothes, hot water for whites or particularly dirty clothes, and warm water for everything in between.

Question

What if the washer or dryer malfunctions?
Sometimes a machine will take your money but not function properly, or something else may go wrong. If there is no service phone number posted in the laundry room, ask your RA how to report the problem. Meanwhile, you still have to finish your laundry, so pick a different machine and try again.

Dryer Safety

Once your load has been washed, you will put it in the dryer. Make it a rule to always empty the lint filter before and after you use the dryer. A clean lint filter allows the dryer to be more efficient, drying your clothes more quickly and completely. Every year there are small fires in laundry rooms that could have been prevented if students had emptied the lint filters. If the dryers are coin operated, be sure to have extra quarters on hand in case a machine takes your money but doesn't work, or the dryer doesn't dry your entire load in the first cycle.

Stains and Other Crises

Whether you're a sloppy eater or just a victim of circumstance, you are likely to find a stain on your clothing, a button missing from your shirt, or a rip in your pants at some point in your college career. While living at home, you likely had a family member who could effortlessly resolve these little crises. But now that you are away at college, you will have to learn to deal with these problems on your own.

When you find a stain on your clothing, first try removing the stain with a small amount of laundry detergent or dish soap. Use cold water and be gentle as you work with the stained area. Many times small stains can be resolved this way and you can toss the clothing in with your next load of laundry. If the stain is more persistent or has set in, you need to pretreat the stained area when you are about to do a load of laundry. You can use a small amount of liquid detergent or a pretreating product to do this. Follow the directions on your stain remover and read cautions carefully in case the remover will not work well with a particular kind of stain or fabric.

 **Essential**

Instead of washing four loads of laundry at once, consider doing two loads one day and the other two a few days later. In doing this, you won't have to drag a ton of heavy laundry down to your laundry room, and you won't risk losing as much clothing to theft or other problems.

LAUNDRY CHECKLIST:

☐ Detergent—be sure you see if your machines use powder or high-efficiency (he) liquids.
☐ Quarters or coin for machines
☐ Bleach or bleach pen to treat whites

☐ Dryer sheets as needed

☐ Stain spray or spotting stick for messy spills

☐ A zipper or cinch top mesh bag for delicates to keep them protected and separate from the larger items and weight of loads

☐ Laundry bag and basket to sort and fold

Campus Laundry Services

One other more costly but very convenient option is to see if your campus offers an off-site, send-your-clothes-out laundry service. Usually the service provides you with a specially labeled bag and assigns a designated pickup and drop-off day and time. These services can be pricey but will save you valuable time! Also, remember these laundry companies are industrial services, so they may not provide special attention to stains or delicate items you send out.

Final Laundry Thoughts

Consider visiting a local Laundromat to see if they offer student specials or even wash-and-fold services and delivery. Also, be sure you stay on top of your laundry by making time to do it at least once a week or it can overtake you.

 **Essential**

A local dry cleaner may be the best answer for clothing crises. If you haven't washed the item, the dry cleaner may be able to remove a stain. Point out the stain and tell the staff what it is (food, paint, etc.). Using this method will give you the benefit of clean, pressed clothing, but remember that you'll have to pay for the service.

Also, if you are an athlete, be sure you see if your school gym can take care of the extra dirty, sweaty team uniforms. Items like socks, Under Armor or sports leggings should be aired out before just balled up into your laundry basket. Perhaps invest in a small drying rack where you can hang wet, damp or sweaty items until they dry and can be moved to your laundry pile or bag. Moist or sweaty items can smell and even mold if left sitting for too long.

Finally if your campus is close to home, don't solely rely on bringing all of your laundry to mom or dad and waiting until you have run out of clean items to do so.

CHAPTER 8

Choosing Classes and a Major

Your primary purpose for going to college is to get an education. You may want that education in order to increase your knowledge, increase your earning potential, or help you serve others. In addition to your formal education, you will learn how to apply knowledge, gain interpersonal skills, and have a tremendous amount of fun. But your central mission is earning a degree, and this is accomplished by completing academic requirements. At college, you alone must ensure that you are taking the proper courses to achieve your goals.

Advisement

Sometime in the summer before you begin classes, you should be assigned an academic adviser. This may be a professor who will be teaching a required first-year student course, a professor who teaches courses in your major, or a member of the academic advising staff.

Your adviser should:

1. Be your personal expert on academic matters
2. Serve as your main consultant about course selections
3. Give you an idea of which classes new students typically select
4. Offer suggestions about classes that will fill requirements or help you explore possible majors
5. Explain the class registration process
6. Help you with reminders about dates and procedures for dropping or adding classes to your schedule

 **Essential**

At some schools, you will register for classes after you arrive on campus and meet with your academic advisor. At other schools, you will register for classes prior to stepping foot on campus. If you fall into the latter category, you must be more assertive about getting the advice you will need to pick appropriate classes.

In addition to your adviser, the suggestions and sources that follow are worth considering for additional advice:

- Ask current students what they think. Students will tell it like it is. They will give you their thoughts and truthful opinions about professors, classes, campus truths and myths, etc.
- Student advisers can tell you what combinations were overwhelming for them or for other first-year students they knew.
- If you don't know a student currently at your college, call the orientation office and ask to speak with a student, or call the admissions office and ask to speak with one of the student tour guides. These students may be less candid than someone you already know, but they can still offer a good perspective.
- Go online to *www.ratemyprofessors.com*, but be cautious about not taking a class simply because one or two students gave the professor a poor rating.

Finally, if you truly believe that you know what you want to do after college, ask a professional in that field what she would recommend. For example, if you want to be a dentist, ask your dentist what she would take if she were starting college again. In addition to possibly gaining some good advice, you're developing a deeper relationship with a person who might be able to give you an internship, summer job, or job recommendation in that field. Part of getting good advice is asking good questions. Think about what you want to accomplish during your college education.

Balance Your Schedule

The list of course offerings you initially receive will include a wide range of classes. Even after you have solicited advice from informed people, and received unsolicited advice from interested relatives and friends, you'll have a number of courses in mind. Some classes are safe bets because you took something similar in high school. If you had two years of Spanish in high school, then taking the introductory Spanish class at college is a safe bet. The college course will still be challenging because it will move at a faster pace and your professor will expect more of you, but your familiarity with the topic will serve you well. However, if the high school and college courses are too similar, you may receive a duplicate experience, and thus waste your time and money. For this reason, it's a good idea to speak with or e-mail the professor before registering for his class.

Other classes might be interesting, but fall completely outside of your academic experience thus far. Astronomy is a fascinating course that might fill a general education requirement, but if you've never taken a similar class, the new material could give you trouble. If there is no prerequisite—a course you must pass before you can take a higher-level course—then the college feels that you are eligible for the class. Don't be afraid to try something new.

Early in your undergraduate career you have the opportunity to be creative with the classes you take. If you are intent on majoring in biology, then you might select a course in pottery or dance as an elective. You will have the opportunity to think in new ways, meet a different group of students, and gain a better-rounded education by experimenting in this way. You will also gain an appreciation for the type of work other disciplines do and a vocabulary that will help you communicate with a wider variety of people.

Essential

New students often get nervous about the academic demands of college. It will be harder, faster, and more demanding than high school. But remember that your college admitted you because they expect you to succeed. Your application showed something about you that they chose to believe in. If experienced professionals believe in you, you have a good reason to believe in yourself.

As your college career progresses, you will have less and less opportunity to take classes outside of your major—do so while you can. Whatever you choose to do, the basic goal is to have a balanced schedule. Pick a few classes that fall within your comfort zone, and pick at least one that represents a challenge or a creative opportunity.

The following list can be used to keep track of classes you're thinking of taking:

Semester: _____

Registration Deadline: _____

Core Requirements:

_____

_____

_____

_____

_____

_____

Major Requirements:

_____

_____

_____

_____

_____

Electives:

_____

_____

_____

_____

_____

_____

Core Requirements

Once you declare a major, there will be a particular set of courses you must complete. Similarly, you may have a set of basic classes, or core requirements, that you must complete in order to earn a degree from your college. Often you can fill a particular requirement by choosing one course from a list within a particular category. For example, in order to complete a cultural understanding requirement, you may be able to choose from several history courses. You can find information about core requirements in your college bulletin/catalog.

Use this list to keep track of the classes you take to fulfill your core requirements:

REQUIREMENT	CLASS	YEAR

REQUIREMENT	CLASS	YEAR

You'll have to make a decision about when to complete your core requirements. One strategy is to complete all core requirements as soon as possible in your college career, leaving your final years to focus on courses in your major. Another approach is to do things in the completely opposite order, focusing on your major initially and completing core requirements in your final semesters of college.

⚹ Question

Do I have to take foreign language classes in college, even if I took them in high school?
Every school has a unique policy on foreign languages. Many schools require you to have taken at least one year of language courses at the college level. Other schools will acknowledge your high school language achievements as sufficient. Some colleges also offer a proficiency exam that gives you a reprieve from taking language classes if you pass it, and some will allow you to take alternative courses to satisfy the language requirement.

For most students, the sensible choice rests somewhere in the middle. Taking one or two core requirement courses each semester keeps you on track for graduation and allows you to take other courses for your major, minor, or personal interest. It's also nice to have one or two less-challenging classes while you're taking the toughest courses in your major. As a senior, you may not be overwhelmed by an introductory course, even if the freshmen in your class are.

Declaring a Major

You may have come to college with a career goal in mind. Or you may know that you will need a college education but are not certain about a major or career. Unless you plan to be involved in a specific preprofessional program, such as premedical, you have some time before you need to declare a major. Your first semesters at college should be spent taking courses in a variety of areas, filling some core requirements, and allowing your interests to develop. Most schools will require you to declare a major no later than the end of your second year or the beginning of your third year.

 **Essential**

It's important to choose a major that interests you, but it should also lead you to a career or graduate program once you graduate. If you only have a general idea of a career that you might enjoy, declare a less-specific major, such as business or communications. This will prepare you for a wide array of jobs and still allow you to further shape your education in graduate school.

If you're uncertain about what your major should be, visit your career center and begin to explore your options. Career centers offer a variety of resources to help students sift through interests, aspirations, possible majors, and potential careers. They can also help you understand how a single major can launch a career in one of several fields, giving you more flexibility and perhaps peace of mind when you declare a major.

If you are having trouble deciding what your major should be try and answer these questions:

What do I love? What am I passionate about? _____

_____

_____

_____

_____

_____

What am I good at? _____

_____

_____

_____

_____

What classes/clubs/courses did I enjoy in high school? _____

_____

_____

_____

_____

Is there anything I've always dreamed of doing? _____

_____

_____

_____

_____

What skills do I want to learn? _____

_____

_____

_____

_____

_____

Do I thrive in a particular kind of environment? _____

_____

_____

_____

_____

_____

Do I prefer working with people? _____

_____

_____

_____

_____

_____

What life situations do I have to keep in mind (i.e., family obligations, cultural aspects, financial obstacles) _____

_____

_____

_____

_____

_____

When you know what your major will be—or at least your first major, since you will be able to change your mind—sit down with your academic adviser and discuss your plans. Your registrar will have the official major declaration form for you to complete.

Minors and Double Majors

Most colleges offer you the opportunity to declare a minor area of study, and some actually require such a declaration. The idea is that you can develop a concentration of knowledge on a particular subject, in addition to your major area of study. Many students who declare minors try to pick something that compliments the major they have chosen. You are best served by choosing a minor in an area of personal interest. The more you enjoy the learning process, the more you will gain from it.

✅ Fact

Your minor will show up on your college transcript, and perhaps your first resume, but after that it is of little interest to potential employers. So, treat your minor as a chance to explore a subject you really enjoy. Try biology or art even if your major is political science. You may discover a lifelong pursuit outside your career.

Many schools also give students the opportunity to declare two simultaneous majors. Termed a double or dual major, this choice allows a student to become an expert in two areas of study.

In the case of minors and dual majors, it's always a good idea to speak with your academic adviser about your interests and plans. You'll want as much help as possible ensuring that you are completing your major and minor requirements as efficiently as possible, keeping up with core requirements, and preparing yourself for a job or graduate school after college. Additionally, consider a visit to the career center. Present the staff there with your ultimate post-college plans and ask for their thoughts about an appropriate major and/or minor.

Studying Abroad

While you are a college student, you can take advantage of the opportunity to visit, study in, and perhaps even live in other parts of the world. Study in another country or away from your home campus is referred to as study abroad, and it sometimes includes programs (called domestic exchange programs) on another domestic campus. Some programs allow you to study the language or culture of another country, and others help you study your major from the perspective of another environment.

🔔 Alert

When planning a trip to study abroad, be certain to visit your financial aid office. Your aid package may not be acceptable to some programs, and if you are going abroad without aid, you need to ensure that your assistance package will still be available when you return. Be sure to speak with your financial aid officer early in the planning process.

Students who study abroad report significant changes in themselves. They see the world differently, have a new understanding of what can be done with a particular major, and often develop a new sense of self. Though going abroad can be scary, it can also enrich your life in ways you never thought possible.

Many colleges have their own study abroad programs or have agreements with colleges that have such programs. If you take full advantage of the opportunity, you will quickly learn the native language and adapt to local customs. Though most students find a new culture to be intimidating at first, immersing yourself in the experience will prove to be very rewarding in the end.

Using a school-sponsored program means:

- The program is approved by your campus and your school has already accredited the classes you will take while abroad. The classes you take away from your campus will transfer back and count toward your degree and graduation requirements.

- Your financial aid package will be least affected by working through a school-sponsored program.
- You will be housed by your school at another university, or set up with an apartment, or you will be hosted by a screened local family.

If your school does not offer a program to a location you desire, you can:

- Find another school that does offer the program you are seeking. (You will have to find out details from the sponsoring school and see if your college can accept the courses and continue to keep you listed as an active student.)
- Try to arrange a study abroad experience on your own. In these cases, you need to work closely with your academic adviser and campus study abroad coordinator.

 **Essential**

Most study-abroad programs will either house you at a university, set you up with an apartment, or arrange for you to stay with a local family. In any case, you will quickly learn the native language and adapt to local customs if you take full advantage of the opportunity. Though most students find a new culture to be intimidating at first, immersing yourself in the experience will prove to be very rewarding in the end.

Summer and Intersession Programs

If you cannot leave campus for an academic year or even a full semester, ask your campus study abroad coordinator about summer opportunities. There are a variety of programs lasting from five to eight weeks in the summer that can give you a solid experience in another country. Many times these programs occur through a course offered on your campus and may involve traveling to several countries. Summer programs still offer you the chance to learn about another country, its culture, and its people. Shorter programs may allow you to have the best of both worlds—study abroad for academic credit and a summer job to pay for the experience.

An increasing number of schools are also developing study abroad programs for intersession or break periods. The month of January is often an opportunity for faculty to take a group of students to another country for a few weeks. This trip is typically done in the context of a particular class, but is usually available to students regardless of their declared major. Sometimes these classes will be interdisciplinary, giving a few professors the opportunity to collaborate on a course in which the students may think broadly about the location and the subject matter.

Study Abroad Checklist

Use this list to compare study abroad programs.

Program: _____

Location: _____

Dates of Program: _____

Deadline for Application/Registration: _____

Transportation Costs: _____

Other Costs: _____

_____

_____

Pros:

_____

_____

_____

_____

_____

_____

_____

Cons:

_____

_____

_____

_____

_____

_____

_____

Program: _____

Location: _____

Dates of Program: _____

Deadline for Application/Registration: _____

Transportation Costs: _____

Other Costs: _____

_____

_____

Pros:

_____

_____

_____

_____

_____

_____

_____

Cons:

_____

_____

_____

_____

_____

_____

_____

Program: _____

Location: _____

Dates of Program: _____

Deadline for Application/Registration: _____

Transportation Costs: _____

Other Costs: _____

_____

_____

Pros:

_____

_____

_____

_____

_____

_____

_____

Cons:

_____

_____

_____

_____

_____

_____

_____

Program: _____

Location: _____

Dates of Program: _____

Deadline for Application/Registration: _____

Transportation Costs: _____

Other Costs: _____

_____

_____

Pros:

_____

_____

_____

_____

_____

_____

_____

Cons:

_____

_____

_____

_____

_____

_____

_____

CHAPTER 9

Time Management

In the past your mom or dad may have helped you with your homework, insisted that you practice your musical instrument, or made sure you went to bed at a decent hour. You parents might have played more of a managerial role to you. As you head off to college, though, your parents likely shift into being more of your consultant. While you're away at college, you alone will be responsible for managing your time. This is not impossible to do, but it's not easy, either. You will likely have to try a number of time management tactics before you discover a routine that works for you.

Create a Master Calendar

Make a calendar to block out your time commitments:

- Start with your class calendar that blocks out the chunks of time you are in class.
- Fill in times of club meetings, team practices, or a job commitment. While these parts of your schedule may be more flexible than your classes, you have a responsibility to your fellow club members, your teammates, and your employer.
- Block out time for your meals based on the openings in your class and extracurricular schedule. Know the college cafeteria hours.
- Be sure you have enough time to sleep. Ideally, allow yourself seven to nine hours of sleep each night. Consider sleep to be a nonnegotiable item in your time management system.
- Schedule your study time in open blocks in the day, in evenings and on weekends. Most colleges recommend at least three hours of study for each hour of class so that students can do the necessary reading, review lecture notes, and prepare for class discussions or presentations. But generally, students find they need to study more for some classes than for others, and they adjust their schedules accordingly.
- Break study time up into sections. Try to keep study blocks to about an hour for each class. You can break up study blocks with other activities or take a short break and begin a study block for another class.

- Look carefully at your schedule and see if there is hidden time that you can use for study as well. For example, if you have class at 10:00 A.M., consider studying for that class each day at 9:00 A.M. right after eating breakfast. Or if the class ends at 11:00 A.M. and you have nothing scheduled until lunch, plan to go to the library and study for that class from 11:00 A.M. to noon. Studying for a class immediately before or after it meets helps you retain the material being covered, and studying during the daytime will allow you more time to relax in the evening.

Essential

A tip for keeping a balanced schedule is to manage your time according to your body's strengths. If you do your best thinking during daylight hours, plan to study then. If you are more of a night owl, you may choose to study in the evening. You should also plan to exercise at a time when you generally have low energy in order to recharge your body.

Balancing a Job

Even though your education and your health should be your main priorities, for most students, a job is necessary to pay for college tuition, books, or other needs. If this is your situation, you need to treat your job just as seriously as you do your classes. When you find a job, consider and practice the following:

☐ Abide by your employer's schedule.

☐ Follow the rules of the institution where you work.

☐ Be respectful of your employer and colleagues.

☐ If you need a job to afford school but find that your current position is too stressful or time-consuming, look for a replacement position where you can work fewer hours.

Unscheduled Events

No matter how many commitments you have, you will need to leave some time unscheduled each day, like having a meal with friends, taking a nap, or watching a movie. If you schedule every minute of every day, you will quickly become stressed out. Here are some ideas for how to build free time into your schedule:

☐ Leave a few empty spaces in your schedule to gain the freedom to adjust things each day, be spontaneous, or just relax. "Doing nothing" is sometimes the only way to gain the composure you need to get through the day.

☐ Plan your weekends, even if you plan them loosely. Saturday is a fine study day, though you should still allow yourself time to sleep-in if you so desire. Sunday afternoons are a good time to do reading for your classes, especially when the weather is nice and you can sit outside somewhere on campus. Sunday evenings are a traditional study time as well. Plan to have

Friday and Saturday evenings free to socialize with your friends.

☐ Schedule small trips home or to visit friends at other colleges when your weekend allows.

✪ Essential

Make a list of the fun things you want to do each month, from seeing movies to attending campus events. Then plug those items into your schedule so that you don't forget them or schedule over them. You won't have time to attend every event or see every movie, but you should be able to fit in your first choices.

Trading Time Blocks

If you give up your hour of biology study to go out with your friends, you need to add an hour of study at a later point in the day or week. Before you head to the movie, determine when you will make up the study time. One strategy is to trade similar time blocks. That is, if you forgo an hour of study to be social, replace an hour of social activity you had planned for later in the week with an hour of study. If you repeatedly skip study time to be social, you will eventually fall behind in your classes.

 **Essential**

Sometimes the key to keeping to your schedule is saying no to friends who want to do other things. Be determined to make your schedule work, and say no to interruptions and distractions. If friends push you, tell them that you will join them when you have finished. Self-discipline is the single most important factor in successful time management.

The challenge is figuring out when to trade a time block and when to decline an opportunity. You should not repeatedly decline social opportunities. If you do, your friends will soon stop asking you to participate in spontaneous trips or events. Similarly, you can't ignore your study schedule every time an opportunity arises. You must identify the type of opportunity and weigh it against your overall schedule.

Combining Tasks

You will have many opportunities to combine tasks while at college, but you have to be selective about which tasks you combine. Writing a term paper while eating dinner may leave a mess on your keyboard or food all over your notes. However, catching up on your reading while you wait for your laundry to dry may be a very efficient use of your time. Multitasking is a common time-management strategy among college students. The challenge is to find tasks that can be successfully combined.

MULTITASKING TIPS

☐ Multitask while doing your laundry. Laundry takes up a lot of your time and there is no way to avoid it. So, while your clothes are in the washer or dryer, do some reading, get ahead on an assignment, or review the notes you took in class that day.

☐ Use laundry time to write your family a letter, fill out birthday cards for friends, or plan your holiday shopping list.

☐ Combine tasks when waiting in line, for the bus, for a ride, in a teacher's office, etc. If you know you will have to endure a waiting period at some point in the day, carry some flash cards or a book with you. Even if you only get through a few cards or a few pages, the wait will go by quicker, and you'll be closer to accomplishing your task.

🔵 Alert

Just as important as your physical health is your mental health. If you begin to suffer from extreme stress or anxiety over your classes or grades, you need to reevaluate your situation and seek the advice of an RA, counselor, or friend. Though while you are in college your goal is to excel academically, nothing is more important than your health.

Planners and Calendars

There are enough planners, calendar systems, and other time-management aids to make a student's head spin. You can literally spend hundreds of dollars on time-management computer software or on books about time management. However, as a student, you will not need or be able to afford such materials. Some students choose to keep track of their time using basic student planners, while others prefer to jot notes on wall calendars. Be sure to consider all of your options before selecting your own time-management strategy.

❶ Alert

Some college students approach time management overconfidently, thinking that they can keep track of everything in their heads. However, just as it is difficult for a waiter to remember several dinner and drink orders without writing them down, most students cannot succeed in college without documenting assignments, appointments, and other plans.

Your word processing program may provide an alternative to purchasing a planner. It probably has a calendar template you can customize and then print out. You can then post a copy over your desk and put one in your notebook. It's important to make your planner visually effective, whether it is a homemade calendar or a store-bought planner. To achieve this, you may want to color-code your schedule or use a highlighter to draw attention to important points.

No matter how you create or customize your planner, the important thing is that you have one, keep it updated, and reference it often.

Some students use their smart phones to store information such as schedules and addresses or use their cell phone to do this. Most phones offer various functions, including phone, camera, e-mail, and music capabilities. One big advantage of most smart phones is the alarm feature. This function can be used to wake you up, remind you about an upcoming meeting or appointment, or alert you to the approach of a deadline.

Essential

Your college will provide you with a calendar of each semester or the entire academic year. This calendar may include dates of final exam periods, seasonal and holiday breaks, and other major events at the college, such as Homecoming weekend. If you have chosen to use a planner to manage your time, be sure to mark it with these important college dates right away.

Check out some online time-management tools such as:

- Free tools for your smartphones: *http://ptmoney.com/15-free-online-time-management-tools*. Here you can find free online to-do lists, calendars, time tracking, project management, and time-management tools.
- Free advice as well on many important college student concerns: *http://blog.gradguard.com*

Cramming Warning

All-night cramming sessions seem to be a rite of passage among college students. Every year students use this method when studying for final exams, but in truth, this strategy is usually far from effective. Losing a full night's sleep will leave you lethargic and unfocused in the morning. When you arrive for your exam, you may have trouble keeping your eyes open, focusing on the page in front of you, or writing coherently. As a rule, don't rely upon cramming.

In most cases, cramming can be (and should be) avoided. If you are using a planner, calendar, app, or other time-management system but are still finding the need to cram for tests, ask your RA, academic adviser, or health center staff for guidance.

The problem may be that you cannot focus on your studies because your residence hall is too noisy or your neighbors are being inconsiderate during exam periods. If this is the case, your RA can seize control over the situation.

If you have simply overloaded your schedule and don't have time to complete your assignments and study for tests, your academic adviser should be able to offer assistance.

And if frequent headaches interrupt your study time, causing you to put it off until the last minute, you may need reading glasses or some kind of medication. Your health center staff may be able to identify such a problem and suggest a solution. Ask for help when needed and heed the advice you receive.

Time Management Checklist

As you try to get your time management skills in order remember the following items:

- ☐ Determine what is the most important to you.
- ☐ Get a calendar (use a whiteboard, online calendar, app for smartphone, etc.).
- ☐ Write down *everything* on your calendar.
- ☐ Don't forget to schedule relaxation times on your calendar.
- ☐ Remember, it's okay to say "no" to some tasks if you can't find time for them. Don't overschedule yourself.
- ☐ If you work, make sure you schedule adequate time to complete your schoolwork before or after your job. School is, after all, your top priority.
- ☐ Allow for flexibility in your schedule.
- ☐ If you find your current calendar system isn't working, try a new system.
- ☐ Don't procrastinate, and plan for the unexpected. What happens if you come down with the flu right when you are planning on writing a paper that's due the next day? What happens if your hard-drive dies? Always try and plan in extra time in case unexpected events arise.
- ☐ Take advantage of unscheduled downtime for studying. Whether you're waiting for a doctor or waiting for your laundry, use that "extra" time to study, and you will be far ahead of the game.
- ☐ Control distractions.
- ☐ Remember to schedule some time for fun!

CHAPTER 10

Effective Study Skills

You need to adopt an effective study routine for everything you do. As a student, you are faced with many tasks, activities, and responsibilities; it can be overwhelming! The key to making it all manageable is making it a matter of habit. The more routine something is, the less effort it requires. Think about your morning routine. You probably go through the same ritual every day—showering, brushing your teeth, and getting dressed—without thinking about it. If you also make study tasks a habit, they'll come as easy as brushing your teeth.

Taking Notes in Class

Much of your time in class will be spent listening to lectures and taking notes. If you do this poorly, your preparations for tests will be difficult and often ineffective. Fortunately, note-taking skills can be easily developed over time and with a little bit of concentration.

When taking notes be sure to consider the following:

- Include the date and overall topic or title of the lecture. This will help you keep information organized when you need to review later.
- Lectures usually have a structure, just like papers you write. There will be an introduction, several main points and illustrations, and a brief summary. When your professor begins her lecture, you want to listen carefully for the structure. Try to identify and write down the focus of the lecture.
- Restate what is being said in your own words. This will help you learn the information more quickly and recall it more accurately later.
- Listen for keywords such as "first" or "for example" that indicate important points or transitions.
- Watch and listen for nonverbal clues about what is important. Your professor's hand gestures, facial expressions, and pauses will add to the material that you are receiving. Some of these clues will help you take notes, indicating which points are more significant than others. Other clues may indicate items that will be on a quiz, related to a paper assignment, or presented on the final exam.

Try to connect what is being said with what you have read outside of class or information that has been covered in previous class meetings. This will help you learn the material, understand what is currently being said, and be prepared for class discussions. Participate in class discussions. This gives you an opportunity to check your understanding of the material with the professor, may help your grade, and lets the professor know that you are an enthusiastic and engaged student.

🔔 Alert

If you know that you are going to miss a class, speak to your professor ahead of time. This will let your professor know that you are interested in the material and are not showing disrespect by your absence. And after absences, never ask your professor: "Did we cover anything important in class?" You should consider all of your classes equally important.

As you take notes, leave the right quarter of the page as a margin, perhaps marking it off as a column. While you are writing your class notes, use this margin to make side comments. Examples of things to write in this margin are:

- Questions about the material being covered
- Indications that the information will be covered on a test
- References to textbooks or other sources
- Concepts you want to revisit for a paper or essay

If you write questions in the margin, it's important to answer them quickly. Do this in your next study session for the class, or approach the professor when the class ends. By the time you get to your next class meeting, all questions should be answered.

As you are taking notes, don't try to write down everything that the professor says. Write down only those points and examples that relate to the topic of the lecture.

Essential

It is important to minimize distractions during class. Don't sit near people who whisper throughout class, always remember to turn your cell phone to vibrate, and try not to sit near windows or doors. If there is a clock in the room, make a point to look away from it so that you can focus on the lecture instead of the time.

Try to take notes in outline or bullet form, relying on single-line entries. Paragraphs will be harder to skim through later when you are looking for a particular piece of information. Use abbreviations to increase your note-taking speed.

Organization Tips

When you're a student, studying becomes your job. But being a student is tougher than some nine-to-five office jobs because your responsibilities and duties are constantly changing. Every day, every week, every month, and every semester present new assignments and tasks, and if you don't keep track of them, you'll find that your work—and your life—become a complete mess.

That's why it's essential that you organize yourself right from the start. Here are some other ways to keep yourself and your life organized.

First, use this checklist to help you address your basic office supply needs:

- ☐ Printer paper
- ☐ File folders
- ☐ Labels
- ☐ Stapler and staples
- ☐ Paper clips and container
- ☐ Pens and mechanical pencils
- ☐ Markers, crayons, poster board, glue stick
- ☐ Highlighters
- ☐ Sticky notes
- ☐ Dry erase board
- ☐ Bulletin board and tacks
- ☐ Scissors, hole punch, staple remover
- ☐ Notebooks, binders, and looseleaf paper
- ☐ Baskets, containers, and mugs to hold desktop items

Then you'll need to organize your study space efficiently so you are set up for success:

- ☐ Keep all of your notes and study materials neatly orga-nized. There's not much point in taking notes if they wind up in a crumpled pile of paper at the back of your desk.

☐ Keep your notes clearly labeled and organized.

☐ Find a space you can designate as your study area, where you keep all the study materials—notes, textbooks, articles—that you need for the semester. That way you'll be able to quickly find anything you need.

☐ Break down larger projects into smaller pieces. For example, if you have a huge book report and presentation to finish, make a timeline and carve the project into pieces with labeled index cards or computer files with names labeling topics such as: introduction, supporting paragraphs, references and bibliography, project visuals, conclusion, examples and illustrations of text, etc.

Come up with a system that works for you, and then repeat it over and over—and fine-tune it along the way as needed.

Study Groups

Studying with a group of friends is not always an effective method of learning material for an exam. While with friends, you may be more tempted to tell jokes than focus on your studies. However, if you exercise discipline, working closely with a small group of others can greatly advance your understanding of a topic and enhance your performance in a class. It's up to you to control experiences when working in groups.

Here are some tips for making a study group work:

- **Maintain a small group.** One to three other students will give you a variety of perspectives, and with only a few members, everyone will have a chance to speak.
- **Choose the study group students carefully.** Seek out students who will take the group seriously, who are generally prepared for class, and who have good class attendance.
- **When your group meets, always have a specific purpose in mind.** You may want to review the last few lectures, discuss the readings, or figure out how certain concepts are related to the focus of the class.
- **The group should work as a team to make sure everyone learns the material thoroughly.** To this end, everyone must participate in the group's discussions.
- **Your location should be comfortable and accessible to everyone in the group.** A residence hall lounge, an enclosed study area in the library, or a local coffee shop where you can remain for several hours if necessary would all be good choices.

 **Question**

What if I can't find a group to study with?
Ask students just before or after class if they are interested in a study group. You can also ask your professor to make an announcement that students interested in joining a group should speak with you right after class. If you're still having trouble, ask your RA or academic advisor for guidance.

Flash Cards

The most effective way to memorize key terms is to work with good, old-fashioned flash cards. Flash cards are particularly helpful when you need to remember a lot of key terms, such as new vocabulary words in a foreign language. Simply take 3" × 5" index cards and write down a term on one side and either a definition, a description of its significance, or a translation on the other.

Although making the flash cards might seem time-consuming, this method has many advantages:

- The process of making the cards helps you begin to memorize the material. As you write down a term and its definition, your mind begins to process the information into your long-term memory.
- Using cards enables you to shuffle and reorganize them in various ways. For example, you can eliminate cards for terms you know well, and continue to test yourself on the ones you don't.
- Flash cards enable you to quiz yourself both ways: You can look at the term and test yourself on the definition or look at the definition and try to guess the term. If you can do both, then you truly know the material. This can particularly help on those questions where you need to furnish the term yourself, such as with fill-in-the-blank questions.
- Flash cards are also useful in preparing for exams on foreign language vocabulary where you need to know either the English definition of a word or the foreign word to answer questions.

Flash cards make it easy for you to test yourself on key terms. Quiz yourself often. Sit with the stack of cards and, for each one, state the definition or description of the term. Then flip the card over to see if you were correct. If you were right and feel pretty confident that you won't forget the term, you can put the card aside. If you got it wrong or had trouble describing it in detail, put the card at the bottom of the stack. Before you do, though, read over the card a few times and make a concentrated effort to remember it. You won't be able to remember something merely because you've read it; you have to make an effort and instruct yourself to remember it.

When you have finished going through the whole stack, shuffle it and start again. Repeat the process, continuing to eliminate any cards you find you know quite well. Eventually you should be able to go through the whole deck and define each term without hesitation. You'll know then that you are ready for the exam.

Effective Reading

Though you will have done a lot of reading in high school, you will have to hone your reading skills yet again in college—you will also be expected to read a lot more material in a much shorter amount of time. Moreover, the information you read will reappear on tests, in class discussions, and in the papers you write. In some cases, you will read books or articles that are never addressed by your professor in class; however, you will still have to understand the key concepts in those readings should they come up on an exam.

The first key to reading at the college level is to initially read the material completely without taking notes or making marks in your book. You need to get a good sense of all the material that is present before evaluating what is or is not important. Remember that this reading may be more complex than what you're used to, so give yourself plenty of time to complete it.

🅔❗ Alert

Reading in bed will only help you do one thing: fall asleep. In order to retain as much material as possible, you should be sitting upright, preferably at a desk, in a well-lit room. If you are reclining in a dim area, you will likely end up using your book as a pillow.

As you are reading, keep several questions in mind. Your professor has a reason for requiring this reading, and if you can identify this reason you will get more out of the reading. This kind of intentional reading will help you learn things more quickly. Examples of questions to keep in mind are:

- What does your professor hope you will gain by reading this material?
- How does the reading relate to what you are covering in class?
- Can you use the information from the reading for an upcoming paper assignment?

- How is this information similar to or different from other things you are reading in this course?
- How does this information relate to things you are reading in other courses?

Study Skills Summary

Here is a quick checklist of things you'll need to do to improve your study skills and succeed in the classroom. Remember this is only a partial list; for a more in-depth look at the skills you'll need to succeed in studying check out *The Everything®* *Guide to Study Skills*.

☐ Find a good system for taking notes in class.

☐ Keep yourself well organized both inside and outside of class.

☐ Form study groups strategically to work to your advantage.

☐ Make flash cards. Practice and use them diligently.

☐ Become a good reader. Read deeply to understand content and relate it back to classwork.

CHAPTER 11

Researching Papers

The ability to do research and present findings in a professional manner is a foundation of the modern college education. The skills you gain during the research and writing process will serve you well for the rest of your life.

Conducting Research

Research is a fundamental part of the college experience, and it's an essential requirement for obtaining most advanced degrees. While it will be time-consuming, it doesn't have to be difficult. As long as you allow yourself enough time to get your work done, you should be able to complete your research thoroughly and write an excellent paper.

Follow these helpful research tips:

- Since the library is the place where you'll conduct most of your research, schedule an orientation to the library. This preliminary measure will save you time and energy whenever you have to conduct research.
- All colleges have a catalog of their holdings. Most schools have placed their catalogs into searchable databases that streamline research. With these systems, you're able to search by author, title, subject, or keyword and have access to databases that will search the holdings of other libraries. For example, WorldCat (*www.worldcat.org*) is an online database that lists the holdings of thousands of libraries.

Alert

If you are going to order something from another library, you may have to wait several days for it to arrive. Taking this into account, you should order all interlibrary loan materials well in advance of your paper's due date. Ordering from another library may also include a nominal fee, so be certain that you really need the item you are ordering.

- Search the Internet for resources related to your topic. Internet searches may yield thousands of results, so be as specific as possible with your searches.
- It is very important to keep track of any source that you consult through notes and citations. You'll have to provide a citation each time you use someone else's ideas, and you'll likely have to include a list of the sources you used when you turn in your paper.
- Professors may also want to know what books and articles you read to prepare your paper even if you don't end up using those sources in your text. Many students use index cards to keep track of sources and quotes. If you use one index card per source, you can easily keep track of the sources you consult.
- Find out your professor's preferred method of citing sources; what particular style guide, and which edition of it, does he prefer? *The Chicago Manual of Style* and the *APA Style Manual* are two examples of style guides. Your college bookstore will have the style guides most often used by professors, or you can find them online. It is a good idea to either purchase one of these books as a reference or purchase an online subscription, especially if your major will require a lot of research and writing.
- As you take notes from books, periodicals, and other sources, take the time to note which source gave you each quote.

Research Is a Process

Don't think of research as a one-time visit to the library or Internet. You'll probably have to make several trips to the library, place multiple orders for books from another library, and consult the Internet on more than one occasion. As you work on your first draft, you'll probably discover that you need to find more information to support a particular point, or that a new point has emerged. If you expect these occurrences from the start, you'll be more flexible when things come up.

 **Essential**

Think of research as detective work. You are essentially investigating your topic in search of clues to reach a result (your final project). Using quotes, facts, and other informative nuggets in your writing, clue your reader into your process and investigative expertise.

There are two kinds of sources: *primary* and *secondary*. Primary sources are any texts that are the focus of an essay, such as specific works of literature, historical documents, or essays and articles that present certain theories and philosophies. For example, if you are writing about some of Shakespeare's plays, then *Romeo and Juliet* and *Hamlet* would be primary sources. If your essay centers on a primary source, you must be certain you read it in detail and take notes on it.

Secondary sources are books and articles by critics, historians, scholars, and other writers who comment on and address primary sources, as well as other topics and subjects. If your essay involves conducting research, you need to track down secondary sources that address your topic and take notes on them.

Where to Find Possible Sources

There are obviously many sources that address your topic, but before you read them, you need to find them. Fortunately, there are several resources you can turn to for help in finding possible sources.

The Online Library Catalog

Almost all libraries list their sources on computer. The entries are usually organized four ways: by author, title, subject, or keywords. If you have a specific source in mind, you can consult either the author or title entries to find out if the library has the source and where it is located. If you are merely looking for general sources, though, you can search according to the subject.

 **Essential**

Become familiar with your library, not just as a quiet space where you can study, but also as a source of information. Finding the perfect quote or just the right reference source can be very exciting and empowering as you achieve academic success.

Most libraries organize their subject catalogs according to the standard list of subjects set by the Library of Congress, although some libraries have their own classifications. The library should have a subject list available for you to consult. Sometimes a subject will be divided into subcategories. Try to find whatever subject or subcategory most closely relates to your topic.

Published Bibliographies and Indexes

There are many published bibliographies and indexes that list books and other sources, such as academic journals and periodic articles, on a particular subject. These bibliographies compile citations for various books and sources. A citation is a listing for a particular source that includes key information about the book, such as the author, title, publisher, and often a brief summary of the source's content.

Here are some of the major bibliographies that might be helpful in your search for sources.

GENERAL SOURCES

- *Books in Print*
- *Essay and General Literature Index*
- *Reader's Guide to Periodical Literature*

ARTS, HUMANITIES, AND LITERATURE

- *Annual Bibliography of English Language and Literature*
- *Humanities Index*
- *MLA International Bibliography of Books and Articles on the Modern Languages and Literatures*

BIOGRAPHY

- *Biography and Genealogy Master Index*
- *Biography Index*
- *Who's Who*

HISTORY

- *Historical Abstracts*
- *International Bibliography of Historical Sciences*

CURRENT EVENTS

- *Facts on File*
- Newspaper Indexes (Check for specific newspapers such as the *New York Times,* the *Wall Street Journal,* etc.)

SCIENCES

- *General Science Index*
- *Social Sciences Citation Index*

Bibliographies and indexes will usually be located in the reference section of the library. To find a bibliography on your topic, you can either ask the librarian for suggestions or consult the online subject catalog.

Lists of Works Cited and Bibliographies in Sources

Most academic books, essays, and journals include their own bibliographies, list of works cited, or suggested further readings. These listings provide sources you might read yourself as part of your research. Each time you read a new book or article, check the author's bibliography or notes to see if there is anything of interest that you can explore next. You can also check the assigned texts for your course.

Computerized Information Resources

Most of the previous indexes, such as the *MLA Bibliography* and the *Reader's Guide to Periodic Literature,* are available via computer catalog or Internet. All libraries have computers set up that enable you to conduct online searches or allow you to log into their city's wireless Internet access via your own laptop.

⚠ Alert

Be cautious about including information you find on sites like Wikipedia. Double check sources and facts you find there. Since Wikipedia is a database of millions of articles that can be updated and edited by anyone with Internet access, be cautious of believing the entire content as truth or fact.

Obviously, the Internet is a valuable tool for finding sources. You can access indexes and bibliographies, and you can also find entire articles from newspapers, magazines, and periodicals. Just be careful of Googling every question you have and relying on Wikipedia for your sources of knowledge. Wikipedia is an open site that allows information to be updated and changed rather easily, so be sure you are certain about information you think may be factual but can actually be edited by the public.

The Librarian

Librarians are the most vital resource in the library; they can provide you with a tremendous amount of help for just about any academic project you pursue. Ask them questions; that's what they're there for. Any good library should offer some, if not all, of the previous resources and services. It's a good idea to wander around your library or take a brief tour to find out exactly what the library offers. Then take advantage of it. If you use the library properly, its resources can make the job of being a student much, much easier.

Keeping Track of Sources

It is important to know how to categorize and document all of your sources when conducting research. You also need to stay organized and have a good system in place to keep track of all the places from where you gather your information. This system ultimately will protect you from the threat of committing plagiarism, whether accidental or intentional.

Alert

Perhaps the most important error to avoid when writing a paper is plagiarism. Plagiarism occurs when you use other people's words without giving them credit. Whether you claim another's words as your own on purpose or by accident, the punishment will likely be the same. This offense could cause you to fail the assignment or even be suspended from your college. Be certain to give credit where it is due when using research in your paper.

Whenever you find a reference to a source you'd like to investigate, make a note of it. It is extremely important that you write down all relevant information: the author(s), title, publisher (for a book); volume and date (for a periodical or journal); or anthology name and editor (for an essay or article included in another work). This information helps you to find the source and is also necessary when you create your own bibliography. You can keep this information in a notebook, on a legal pad, or in a file on your laptop.

Taking Notes

When you are reading a particular source, you may not be certain what to take notes on. Sources can be quite long; how do you know what is relevant and what isn't? The most important thing to look for is anything that supports your thesis statement. Essentially, you are looking for hard evidence that argues in favor of your thesis. You can also take notes on anything that relates to your general topic, since these notes will help you develop broad background knowledge of the field and might be used in the essay. Also, take notes on anything that intrigues you or sounds interesting. You won't necessarily use all of these notes in the essay, but it is much easier to take notes and throw them out later than to have to reread sources.

✹ Essential

There are many ways to take notes. The simplest method is to use a notebook or legal pad as you read. Some students prefer to take notes directly onto a laptop or desktop computer. Find a system that works for you. Remember to indicate clearly which source the notes come from and their page numbers.

There are two types of notes: *quotations* and *paraphrases*. A quotation restates a passage or a part of a passage from a source in the original writer's *exact words*. A paraphrase, on the other hand, restates the ideas in a passage rephrased in *your own* words.

Quoting

When you are reading a source and come across a sentence or passage you think is relevant, decide whether you want to quote it or paraphrase it. You should generally paraphrase more often than you quote. It is too tedious and time-consuming to copy down long passages word for word. If a sentence or passage is written in a particularly interesting or powerful manner that you think will stand well on its own in the essay however, copy it as a quotation.

Be certain you enclose copied lines in quotation marks. To be certain you remember that the note is a quotation, you may even want to write "Quotation from Original" next to the line in parentheses. If you want to leave out part of a quotation because it is not relevant, you can use an ellipsis to indicate a word or phrase has been deleted. Sometimes, when you take a quotation out of context, it won't make sense on its own and will need some clarification. If you decide to add a word or phrase to the quotation, you must put it in brackets to indicate that the addition is not part of the quotation.

Paraphrasing

If you decide to paraphrase the source, you must rephrase it *completely in your own words*. Make sure that your paraphrase is an accurate restatement of the passage.

Occasionally, you will want to quote a few words or a particular phrase within a paraphrase. You can paraphrase the gist of the passage and include only a few words and phrases in quotation marks. For example, if the author has coined a particular term or described something in a unique way, you can quote those words exactly.

Whenever you take quotes from a source, and even if you paraphrase them, you need to note the source and its exact page number(s). It is important that you do this carefully, as you must include this information later in the essay. If you don't acknowledge the original source, you are committing *plagiarism*, which is considered a serious breach of ethics that can get you expelled from school.

Using Note Cards

If you are utilizing many sources and taking many notes, the material can become difficult to manage. A more efficient and organized means of taking notes is to use note cards. These give you more flexibility—you can shuffle and reorganize them into various groups, or put aside those you decide not to use.

Take notes on index cards (you may want to use a slightly larger size, such as 4" × 6", so you can fit more notes). On each card, write down a particular piece of information from one specific source. Each card should contain a single, specific idea. Copying lengthy quotations and paraphrasing large chunks of text take away the flexibility that note cards provide you with in the first place. Try to limit each card to a single point.

Alert

Keep careful records with complete publication information of all your sources. In order to credit the sources, you need to place a "works cited" page at the end of your essay that includes all this information. Using works cited note cards is the most efficient way to keep track of sources. Simply keep one notecard per source, complete with all its bibliographic information. Alphabetize them at the end and format properly depending on the type of publication source it is: a book, website, periodical, speech, etc.

As long as you have made a works cited card, you don't need to put the full title and complete publication information on each note card. Simply copy down the last name of the author in the upper left-hand corner of the card. If you are using more than one source by a particular writer, you can write down the author's last name and a keyword from the title. In the top right-hand corner, write down the exact page number from which the noted quotation or paraphrase comes.

For those students who don't want to take the traditional index card route, you might want to check out mobile applications and online options to help you keep your notes in order. These sites offer computerized approaches to the old school index card system. Explore your various options and see what works for you. Here are a few sites you can consider:

- Quizlet.com
- Studyblue.com
- Flashcardexchange.com
- Flashcardmachine.com

Plagiarism 101

As you research and generate your own ideas, it's vital to avoid plagiarism. Whenever one writer uses another writer's ideas or words and does not give the original writer credit, it is considered plagiarism. Plagiarism is like stealing. Committing plagiarism is a breach of ethics that can have serious repercussions for a student, including a failing grade or being expelled.

The most blatant form of plagiarism is copying an entire essay from another student or source. It is also considered plagiarism if you include information from another source within your essay and don't credit the source. Even one uncredited sentence or phrase can be considered plagiarism. You probably won't be expelled over one or two uncredited sentences, but failing to document sources can lower your grade or discredit you as a student. This offense could cause you to fail the assignment or even be suspended from your college. Be certain to give credit where it is due when using research in your paper.

Finally, professors have easy access to sophisticated plagiarism detection software, so don't fool yourself into thinking you will be the one to get away with it. Committing plagiarism is an infraction that can haunt your academic record and academic reputation for years and often becomes a part of your permanent academic record. It is so much better to be conservative and cite anything that is not your own work, idea, or quotation than to risk getting tagged as a plagiarist.

CHAPTER 12

Writing a Paper

Before lawyers go to court, they carefully prepare how they intend to present their evidence. They think about the order in which they plan to call up witnesses and the particular lines of questioning they will follow. Planning ahead in this way guarantees an organized and strategically effective presentation of the case. Your paper similarly represents an argument—this one in support of your thesis. You also need to plan ahead, organizing your evidence and devising a presentation strategy.

Plan Your Attack

The first thing to do before you start the writing process is to read through and evaluate all your note cards. Decide which notes are necessary for your argument. You may ultimately decide to put many unrelated notes aside; don't let this bother you. By evaluating notes in a critical manner, only the most powerful material remains. Information that doesn't contribute significantly weighs down the essay and detracts from the stronger ideas.

As you work, keep your own ideas in mind. You may want to use them as the basis for grouping together the themes. Each group of note cards you wrote represents a point you plan to make in the paper. You need to decide next on the order in which you will address these points. Many students follow some variation of the following steps of the writing process.

Brainstorm

You can brainstorm on a blank sheet of paper or computer screen some of your ideas and see how they come together.

- **Try "clustering."** Some students like to "cluster" to come up with a more formal outline. "Clustering" is a visual way of mapping out your future essay. If your essay is about water, for instance, write the word "water" in the center of a page. Then, branching out around it, like the rays of a sun, write various words or terms that support, define, or relate to the topic of water.

- **Try freewriting.** Another technique that can get your structure on paper is freewriting. This is simply a stream-of-consciousness way to get ideas down as they jump into your head. Ignoring sentence structure, grammar, and spelling, just write without stopping until you empty your head of your ideas for your paper.

Start an Outline

In planning your paper, it helps to make a rough outline. The outline simply lists the major points of the essay, and the smaller topics and issues that relate to each one, in the order in which you plan to address them. This gives you a clear map to follow when you sit down to write. Like all good maps, it will keep you from getting lost.

Fact

Always use the "Rule of Three." Due to the way human brains process information (through pattern recognition), three is the preferred number to use when trying to convince someone of something (think of all of the threes in your life: Three Little Pigs; Three Musketeers; blood, sweat, and tears, etc. . . .). For great writing and speaking success, organize your outlines in multiples of three!

Here are some outline tips:

- Try to include as much detail as possible within the rough outline. The more specifics you include, the more organized you'll be.
- Beneath the general categories in the outline, you can mention specific notes from sources you plan to use; you might even want to write out or sum up specific quotations.
- When organizing your points, make sure that you order them in a logical fashion. You want one point to lead to the next so that the reader will be able to follow your argument without having to fill in gaps.
- Certain categories of notes should follow one another. The order in which you raise points can influence the effect they have on your reader.
- Consider how to order your points so that the most persuasive ones pack the most punch.
- Don't start off with a weak point that will make a poor first impression.

Remember that this rough outline is not written in stone; you can make changes at any time. In the process of writing the essay, or after you've read over early drafts of it, you may find that certain points work better if addressed in a different place. You can make as many changes as you like, provided that everything in the essay still relates to the thesis.

 **Essential**

Think of your outline as a table of contents for your paper. It will show anyone, at a glance, what the paper will cover. Throughout the research and writing process, keep your outline where you can see it. Doing so will help you keep the big picture in mind, as well as help keep your thoughts organized.

Write the First Draft

Good writing takes time and effort to produce. You can't expect to get your paper right on the first try and, in fact, you shouldn't even try. Instead, it's better to write in stages, making changes and improvements with each draft.

ROUGH DRAFT GOALS:

- Get all your ideas on paper, and integrate them with notes from other sources.
- Don't concern yourself with correct grammar and spelling in your first draft. This eliminates a great deal of the stress about writing; you don't have to think about the "rules" at first and can simply concentrate on conveying your ideas.
- Start at the beginning of the rough outline and simply start writing. Do your best to explain each of the points. As you need to, refer to your notes and include quotations or paraphrases from other sources.

- Be sure to add citations for each sentence that includes information from another source.
- Keep on writing until you've reached the end of the rough outline. Don't stop to go back and make changes.
- If you hit a roadblock—a point when you freeze and don't know how to proceed—mark the place with an X and move on to another point. You can go back to the trouble spot later.

This first draft will be extremely rough; the writing will be choppy and difficult to read. But that's okay—it's only the first draft and you are the only one who has to see it. This draft provides you with the raw material for your essay; you can then work on it and refine it until it is a real gem.

The Structure of Your Paper

Although there are many ways to structure a paper, the most basic structure includes an introduction with thesis statement, a number of supporting paragraphs, and a conclusion. It is not a law that you have to use this structure for everything you write. You might, for example, have a teacher who is open to more loosely structured essays and who encourages you to be creative. Regardless, this structure is a basic fundamental formula that—if you master it—can take you through college quite effectively. It ensures that the paper remains focused on a specific point and that ideas are presented in a logical and organized fashion. Following this structure, especially when you are first learning how to write academic papers, will help you write more persuasively.

The Introduction

The introduction, at the beginning of the paper, is where you introduce your general topic, specific thesis statement, and approach or methodology. For most papers, the introduction only needs to be a single, well-written paragraph (though for papers twenty-pages or more in length, you may need a longer introduction since there is more ground to cover and a larger set of topics to introduce).

The introduction should draw your reader into your argument right away. It functions somewhat like a movie preview, to give your audience a taste of what's to come, but not the whole story. You want your reader to be enticed and interested in what you have to say.

🅰️ Alert

Remember that whoever is reading your paper probably has to read several others as well. Make your introduction stand out among the others by making it interesting and intriguing. It should not be a long-winded summation of everything you will cover in your paper but rather an enticement to read on.

Your introduction must include your thesis statement. You generally can't begin an essay with the thesis statement itself, because it represents a specific point of view about a broader subject. The introduction sets up the thesis by presenting general background information that gives it a context.

Here are some introduction pointers:

☐ Begin the introductory paragraph with a broad, general statement about the paper's topic, or even consider opening the paragraph with a question. Try to make it interesting and catchy to encourage your reader to want more information. Remember that the first few sentences give the reader the first impression of your essay; it is extremely important that you make a good one.

☐ The first sentences should be well written, interesting, and, most important, give the reader some idea of the paper's topic. The rest of the introduction then bridges the opening statement with the thesis statement, which is usually the last sentence of the introduction.

Essential

Look on your bookshelf at classic titles or go online to read the opening phrases of celebrated books for inspiration on how to begin your paper or assignment. Don't be afraid to take risks in finding creative ways to hook your reader.

☐ The introduction is the first and possibly only place in the essay where you spell out the thesis statement directly for the reader. You therefore need to be careful about how you word it. You don't want it to be too fancy, flashy, or wordy; the power of the idea should be enough to impress the reader. Just state it in a direct, unambiguous manner.

☐ The introduction should come entirely from you. In general, it is not the place to quote and paraphrase outside sources. Those sources belong in the body of the paper, where you use them to prove the thesis statement. It wouldn't make any sense to discuss such specific sources before you've even stated the argument of the essay. Moreover, you want the reader to be primarily impressed by the power of your own ideas.

☐ You can consider beginning with a quotation from another source or by mentioning a specific source, but only if the quotation or source is obviously closely connected to your thesis statement. If the quotation or source introduces specific issues, you probably should not raise it this early in the paper.

The Body

The body is the bulk of your paper; this is where you present your detailed argument that supports the thesis statement. After having conducted research and thought at length about your topic, you should have several points to make. You will therefore use the body to present your ideas in as clear and organized a fashion as possible.

If you have conducted research from primary or secondary sources, you can quote and paraphrase from these sources extensively in this section. Information that comes from other sources serves as strong evidence, but take care to distinguish your own ideas from those in other sources. Quotations and paraphrases should only be brought into the essay to lend credence to your own ideas. Whenever you introduce information from another source, you should explain exactly how it fits in with your own point. And always make sure that each time you quote or paraphrase an outside source, you formally credit the source.

To be effective, your body matter must do three things:

The Material Should Clearly Relate to the Thesis

The most important thing to keep in mind when writing the body of the paper is that every bit of information you include should relate to the thesis, and you must spell out exactly how it does so. If something doesn't relate to the thesis, get rid of it; it's only clouding up your argument, serving as "fluff," and detracting from its power.

Your Arguments Should Be Complete

Because your ideas make sense to you, you may think you have fully explained them, when in fact you haven't done so in a manner that someone else can understand. The reader cannot see inside your head. You must therefore explain all your points carefully, making them clear to the reader. Don't worry at first if it seems that you are over-explaining your points and ideas. It may seem that way to you, but a reader requires a more detailed explanation in order to understand your points as clearly as you do. If you find repetition later upon reading over your draft, you can trim at that point.

🅔✔ Fact

As you write, make sure your paragraphs aren't too long. Long paragraphs weigh down your reader and can be tedious if you drone on and on about a supporting idea. Sprinkle in quotes or even a question to help provide a pause.

Your Writing Should Flow Smoothly

As the writer, it's your job to act as the guide for the reader. As you ease the reader through the complexities of your argument, journeying from one point to the next, you want to create as smooth a path as possible, so that by the end of the paper, the reader won't feel disoriented. At times, you need to make it clear exactly where the paper is heading or summarize what has already been demonstrated. You also don't want the paper to be choppy or difficult to read. Instead, one idea or point should flow smoothly into the next.

One way you can ensure the paper is clearly organized is by focusing each paragraph around a specific point. The body should always be written in paragraphs, not in one long chunk of text. Each paragraph should focus upon a specific point, and every sentence in that paragraph should relate to it. Any sentence in the paragraph that doesn't should be taken out. It's also a good idea to begin each paragraph with a topic sentence that generally introduces the subject matter or main idea of the paragraph.

Each sentence and paragraph in the body should flow smoothly and logically from one to the next. Use transitional words and phrases—such as *similarly, likewise, in contrast, in other words,* etc.,—in certain sentences, particularly topic sentences, so that your reader can easily follow how different points are related to one another.

The Conclusion

After reading the body and all the evidence you've presented in support of the thesis, the reader should now view the thesis statement not as conjecture but as a claim that is supported. That's exactly what you express in the conclusion. The conclusion is essentially the mirror image of the introduction, but one that stresses the fact that the thesis has now been proven. The conclusion should therefore refer to the thesis statement in some form, and affirm that it has been proven and supported. You should also recap the major points you've made in the paper to establish your argument.

Like the introduction, the conclusion only needs to be one paragraph and it should primarily represent your own words and ideas. This is also not a place to quote or paraphrase extensively from secondary sources.

The most basic conclusion inverts the structure of the introduction, starting off with a restatement of the thesis statement, followed by more general statements that sum up the paper's main ideas. The final sentence is a broad remark about the subject or topic.

 **Essential**

While the introduction contributes to the reader's first impression of your paper, the conclusion will influence the reader's final impression. You want to end with a bang—with some of your most powerful and dramatic writing—that leaves the reader absolutely convinced of the validity of your argument.

Polishing a Rough Draft

Once you have gotten your thoughts down on paper, it's time to take a break. Set your paper aside for a few hours or a full day, work on assignments for other classes, or go get some exercise. Once you have had some time away from your writing, come back and read through your rough draft. The first things you want to look for are the main ideas and their adherence to your thesis statement. Questions you should ask yourself at this point include:

- Does the organization of the paper make sense?
- Do the ideas flow easily from one to another?
- Does each section support your thesis?
- Is any important information missing?
- Will a reader who is not familiar with the subject understand your points?

Make sure all your ideas are clearly and fully explained in your paper—that nothing is ambiguous or partially stated, that there are no gaps in the discussion. Examine the organization of the paper and be certain that one point flows smoothly and logically into the next. You might try moving sections around to see if they work more effectively somewhere else. Check that everything in the paper supports the thesis statement, and take out anything that detracts from the argument.

✪ Essential

If you feel comfortable, give your paper to a close friend, mentor, or teacher other than the one who assigned the paper to you. Sometimes fresh eyes can make you see things you missed or may not have considered. Conversely, beware that too many reviewers can take your voice out of the work you created. So pick and choose the feedback you receive and do not second-guess yourself or your instincts.

When you are reviewing your essay, check to make sure you have met the page requirements set by your teacher. Remember, choosing the right topic from the start is the best way to ensure your paper will be the appropriate length. Once you've started writing, you may find your paper is a bit longer or shorter than you intended. If your paper is only half a page longer or shorter, most professors will still accept it. If it is off by more than half a page, then you need to make adjustments.

✅ Fact

If you've included quotations and paraphrases from outside sources, you should also double-check the citations. Make sure you've given each source credit and followed the right format, according to the professor's preferred style guide.

After you have made all the necessary adjustments, it's time to go through your paper line by line, looking for spelling errors, poor sentence structure, and punctuation mistakes. Many computer word processing programs will automatically help you identify possible errors, but always trust your dictionary and style guide over the word processor. Read through your paper, perhaps reading it out loud, in order to find errors.

You should polish your paper several times before you turn it in. Each time you make a correction or incorporate new ideas into the paper, reread it, searching for errors or confusing sections. By the time you finish, you may feel that you are able to recite your paper verbatim, but this important process of revision will help ensure that you have done a thorough job.

Turning in a paper that is not carefully edited makes a very poor impression on a teacher. It indicates that you don't take your work all that seriously. Even if the ideas within the essay are good, not taking the time to edit can lower your grade significantly. Make sure you take the time to edit and that you do it carefully.

Proofread! Proofread! Proofread!

Always proofread your paper before turning it in. When you proofread, you are looking for errors specifically in grammar, spelling, and punctuation. It can often be difficult to catch them because, having looked at the paper so many times, you simply may not see them. In order to proofread effectively, you need to read in a much more focused manner.

PROOFREADING TIPS

☐ If you feel comfortable, give your paper to a close friend, mentor, or teacher other than the one who assigned the paper to you. Sometimes fresh eyes can make you see things you missed or may not have considered.

☐ Conversely, beware that too many reviewers can take your voice out of the work you created. So pick and choose the feedback you receive and do not second-guess yourself or your instincts.

☐ When you are ready, print out a clean copy of the paper. Yes, print it! Printing your paper and reading the hard copy makes it easier to see mistakes that you may not catch on your computer screen. Bring your clean, printed copy to a location where there are absolutely no distractions. It is extremely important that the entire time you read, you keep foremost in your mind that you are trying to locate errors. If you forget this and get caught up in the content of the essay, you will continue to overlook mistakes.

☐ Read slowly and methodically, concentrating on each word and sentence. It is extremely helpful to read out loud, so that you can hear each word; you can also simply mouth the words silently. Hearing your words out loud also helps you identify where you may need extra commas, semicolons, or sentence breaks, too.

☐ Your computer's spell checker program is helpful and can correct many errors, but it doesn't catch everything, nor does it understand the misuse of a word. The spell checker will not catch homophones—words that sound the same but are spelled differently and have different meanings. You should always proofread yourself at least once after you've spell checked your paper.

☐ Sit with a dictionary in hand while proofreading, or keep an online dictionary site open on your computer. Get in the habit of looking up the definition of words you don't use frequently in conversation. In the process of writing and attempting to sound sophisticated, it is easy to use a word you think means one thing when it actually means something quite different.

After you've completed editing, proofreading, and formatting the essay, print out the final version and turn it in!

🅔❗ Alert

Spell-check and grammar checking mechanisms built into your computer's word processing software do not catch every error. So don't rely solely on a computer to find your mistakes. Printing out your paper and reading a hard copy makes it easier to see mistakes that you may not catch on your computer screen.

CHAPTER 13

Internships and Summer Jobs

For most college students, summer is the longest break of the academic year. It's a long enough break that even after a vacation, you'll still have to find something productive to do with the remainder of your time. However, the job you had during high school may no longer suffice. It probably won't help you build your resume, and it may not pay as much as other opportunities. An internship or more focused summer job will help you pursue your career goals and will provide you with valuable life experience.

Meaningful Work

As a college student, your summer experience must include two things: It must be meaningful, and it should make you some money. Your summer experience must be meaningful. You must do something more than you have done in past summers, something that will further your academic or career interests. At the end of the summer, your resume should be stronger and you should be a more attractive candidate to a future employer.

You also need to make money. College expenses extend far beyond tuition, meals, and books. After a year of college, you'll have an idea of how much money you need to earn during the summer. Ideally, you'll also be building a savings account to help you get established after graduation.

Question

What is an internship?
Internships are experiences that connect worksite experience with academic studies. You may be able to get academic credit for an internship, or you may receive a salary or stipend. Internships are available during the summer as well as the academic year. For more information about internships, check with your college's career center.

The ideal situation is a paid internship. A paid internship gives you the experience you want and a paycheck to cover your needs. However, be prepared for that paycheck to be small. A second job may be a good idea, even if the internship is paid. The more money you can earn over the summer, the better. Or, maybe your internship will allow you to earn academic credit; the career counselor or your academic adviser can help you work out the necessary details. You'll need an official faculty sponsor and will probably have to complete some papers or keep a journal in order to receive credit for your work.

Whether or not you have an internship, if you have to get a job just for money, work hard to find something more meaningful than you have had in past summers. Internships are experiences that connect worksite experience with academic studies. You may be able to get academic credit for an internship, or you may receive a salary or stipend. Internships are available during the summer as well as during the academic year.

Internship Basics

One of the first steps in getting an internship is deciding what type of internship you'd like. Then make a list of what you'd like to gain from the internship. Many companies have their interns doing menial tasks like sorting mail or fetching Starbucks orders and these experiences will not necessarily teach you much. You want to have a set goal for what you hope to gain from your internship.

Think about what types of companies would interest you for an internship experience. Would you prefer a large company or a small one, a nonprofit or a *Fortune* 500? Think about what kind of industry will meet your needs and goals.

Next, you'll want to make sure your resume and cover letter are in good shape. You will need to send these important documents to companies where you want to intern, so make sure they are updated and professional looking.

Additionally if you get called in for an interview, dress professionally and come prepared. Your professional appearance and attitude will go a long way to helping companies see you as a viable candidate who is vested in their company. Also, be sure to bring with you an extra copy of your resume, any reference letters you may have, as well as a list of questions you have to ask at the conclusion of your interview.

When interviewing, be prepared to answer these types of questions:

- What experience do you bring to this position (if any)?
- Why do you want to work for our organization?
- What do you hope to gain in your time here?
- What hours can you commit and for how many weeks or months?
- Do you have any personal references you can provide or people who can vouch for your character?
- Why does this industry/company interest you?

Also, be prepared to ask questions of your own such as

- Who will be teaching me or what will I learn here?
- What will my job functions be? Can I sit in on meetings or listen in on phone calls? Will this internship be exclusively

a shadowing opportunity or will I also be able to contribute some of my thoughts?

- How many other interns will be working at the same time as I am?
- What are the specific hours and are there ever weekend or evening hours?
- Is this a paid or unpaid internship? Do unpaid internships ever grow into paid jobs?

Also, be sure to write a thank-you note to your interviewer after your meeting. They will appreciate that personal touch. And follow up in a week if you have not heard back from them about your qualifications or placement for the job.

Finding Internships

Internships are typically not as well advertised as regular job openings so you may have to do some research to find one that is right for you. Check with your college's career center for meaningful internships. Look for positions that involve supervising others or taking on significant responsibilities. (Also ask them for help putting together your resume and cover letter, targeting your desired job, and helping you prepare for the interview.)

Check with an alumni clearinghouse whereby alumni offer opportunities to current students. One reason that alumni work with undergraduates is their passion for the college. They valued their experience at the college and want to help other students. After you work with an alumnus, send him a postcard depicting a scene from the campus. If the experience was particularly helpful, consider sending a souvenir from the bookstore along with a thank-you note. Keep in touch with alumni that you meet through internships or volunteer networks. Once you've graduated, they may be able to help you network your way into your first job.

✪ Essential

Do not wait until the last minute to schedule an appointment with the career center. It might take a few weeks before you are able to be seen, and your career counselor will want to meet with you a few times to ascertain your interests and strengths before suggesting potential internship opportunities or summer job possibilities.

Professional organizations also offer internships. Both the Student Affairs Administrators in Higher Education (NASPA) (formerly, the National Association of Student Personnel Administrators) and the American College Personnel Association (ACPA) are examples of professional organizations that sponsor internships.

Other places you might find internships include:

☐ **Career Fairs:** many colleges, community colleges, community centers, and even high schools host career fairs. Check to see if any local career fairs are in your area. Typically these are events where booths of potential employers are set up. They may be looking to hire but also could be interested if they were approached by potential interns. Don't be afraid to put yourself out there.

☐ **Cold Calling/Cold Contacts:** If an industry interests you, don't be afraid to call, e-mail, write, or even stop by to see if they have interest in interns. Again, you need to be your own advocate. Many companies will be excited for young, bright students to intern at their companies.

☐ **Internship Directories and Websites:** Your library on campus or in your town may have bound directories for internship listings, but you can also explore options and databases on the Internet at sites like: *http://intern ships.com, http://internjobs.com, www.idealist.org, www .experience.com,* and *www.wetfeet.com.*

As you look at internship possibilities, keep a list of the ones that interest you.

Internship Title: _____

Company: _____

Location: _____

Contact Information: _____

Application Deadline: _____

Compensation: _____

Hours: _____

Duties:

_____

_____

_____

_____

_____

Job Requirements:

_____

_____

_____

_____

_____

Notes:

_____

_____

_____

_____

_____

_____

Internship Title: _____

Company: _____

Location: _____

Contact Information: _____

Application Deadline: _____

Compensation: _____

Hours: _____

Duties:

_____

_____

_____

_____

_____

Job Requirements:

_____

_____

_____

_____

_____

Notes:

_____

_____

_____

_____

_____

_____

Internship Title: _____

Company: _____

Location: _____

Contact Information: _____

Application Deadline: _____

Compensation: _____

Hours: _____

Duties:

_____

_____

_____

_____

_____

Job Requirements:

_____

_____

_____

_____

_____

Notes:

_____

_____

_____

_____

_____

_____

Internship Title: _____

Company: _____

Location: _____

Contact Information: _____

Application Deadline: _____

Compensation: _____

Hours: _____

Duties:

_____

_____

_____

_____

_____

Job Requirements:

_____

_____

_____

_____

_____

Notes:

_____

_____

_____

_____

_____

_____

If you're not able to find a meaningful job or internship for the summer, look for service opportunities. Volunteering to work with a local shelter or hospital can be extremely rewarding and translate into an excellent entry on your resume. These experiences can profoundly affect how you view the world and give you a sense of accomplishment. Consider volunteering with a local youth program as well. Serving as a coach or instructor can be a lot of fun, is good for your resume, and will give you the opportunity to improve a young person's life.

Reflections on Your Experience

In grade school, many students spend the first day of school talking about what they did for summer vacation. Some students have to write short essays about their experiences. In college, the experience is similar but the reasons are different. When you are putting together your next resume, the career counselor is going to ask you what you did for the summer and what you learned from the experience. Your academic adviser may ask you the same thing. Keep a weekly journal to record your experiences. Writing down a few sentences on a regular basis can help you recall important events and demonstrate to yourself how much you learned from the experiences.

Keep a copy of the job description and make notes of additional responsibilities you had. At the end of the summer, take some time to write down what you learned from the summer and how you think it benefited (or didn't benefit) you.

Here are some things to keep track of in your journal:

- ☐ Internship title
- ☐ Supervisor
- ☐ Major duties
- ☐ New skills learned
- ☐ Contacts made
- ☐ Favorite part of the job
- ☐ Least favorite part of the job
- ☐ Unexpected benefits of the experience
- ☐ Overall impression of the experience

When career counselors or advisers ask you about the summer, you want to have a thorough and interesting answer to give. Your journal will be a good reference tool for you. However, if your answer isn't polished, these people will help you sort through what you did and what it all means. They can also help you make connections between your summer experiences, your academic work, and your career goals.

APPENDIX A

Internet Resources for College Students

There are numerous fun and useful websites for college students. From buying textbooks to keeping in touch with family at home, there are resources on the Internet to help you with virtually any task or problem. Though you will certainly discover others during your college career, here are some Internet resources to give you a head start.

Academics

Sparknotes
A collection of study guides, including literary and nonliterary topics
www.sparknotes.com

Rate My Professor
Student ratings of professors at colleges around the country
www.ratemyprofessor.com

Chegg.com's Homework Help
Online homework help for many majors, 24/7
www.chegg.com/homework-help

Alternative Spring Break

Break Away
Many alternative spring break opportunities
www.alternativebreaks.org

Live United
Alternative spring break opportunities offered through the United Way charities
www.liveunited.org/take-action/alternative-spring-break

Jewish National Fund
Alternative spring break trips for Jewish students
www.jnf.org/asb

Finding Dulcinea
This site provides a guide to alternative spring break programs around the world
www.findingdulcinea.com

Humor and Games

The Onion
A critically humorous news source
www.theonion.com

FARK.com
Aggregator of obscure and unbelievable news stories
www.fark.com

Sporkle
Games, entertainment, and trivia
www.sporkle.com

Stumble upon
A personalized browsing tool to help you find interesting websites
www.stumbleupon.com

Mini Clip
Online games site
www.miniclip.com

College Humor
Amusing pictures, movies, and games
www.collegehumor.com

Mad Blast
Movies, music, television, and games that parody popular figures
www.madblast.com

JibJab
Political parodies and cartoons
www.jibjab.com

eBaum's World
"Media for the masses"—jokes, games, videos, and cartoons
www.ebaumsworld.com

Homestarrunner
Popular online cartoon
www.homestarrunner.com

Bored.com
Dedicated to procrastination and entertainment, with games, media, and links
www.bored.com

Milk and Cookies
Games and humorous news stories
www.milkandcookies.com

Personal Space on the Web

Xanga.com
"The Weblog Community"
www.xanga.com

Livejournal
A site for online journals
www.livejournal.com

Angelfire
Provides free web space
www.angelfire.lycos.com

Webs.com
"The next generation of free web hosting"
www.webs.com

Movies and Music

IMDb
The Internet movie database
www.imdb.com

Netflix
Online streaming or DVD rentals
www.netflix.com

Sidereel
TV and movies online
www.sidereel.com

OVG
Online video guide
www.ovguide.com

TV Duck
Free movies and TV online
www.tvduck.com

Hulu
Free movies and TV online
www.hulu.com

CMJ
"New music first"; music reviews, reports, and news
www.cmj.com

Pollstar
Popular music resource
www.pollstar.com

Allmusic
A place to explore new bands or genres
www.allmusic.com

Allmovie
Film and actor reviews and movie sales
www.allmovie.com

Textbooks

Amazon.com
Books, including new and used textbooks, and other products
www.amazon.com

Barnes and Noble
Books, including new and used textbooks, and other products
www.barnesandnoble.com

Half.com
An eBay partner site with new and used textbooks, as well as other products
www.half.ebay.com

efollet
Online location of a popular college bookstore
www.efollet.com

Bigwords
Helps students find the best deals on textbooks
www.bigwords.com

Chegg
Low-cost textbook rental site
www.chegg.com

Travel

Student Universe
A place to find cheap domestic and international flights, as well as resources for traveling in Europe
www.studentuniverse.com

Lastminute.com
A resource for travel within Europe
www.lastminute.com

EasyJet.com
Cheap travel within Europe and helpful to students studying abroad
www.easyjet.com

Expedia Travel
Flights, cruises, hotels, and travel packages
www.expedia.com

Orbitz Travel
Flights, cruises, hotels, and travel packages; Expedia competitor
www.orbitz.com

Southwest Airlines
Great prices if they travel to the vicinity of your destination
www.southwestairlines.com

Hostels Worldwide
Search over 25,000 hostels in more than 180 countries
www.hostelworld.com

Cheapo Air
The name says it all
www.cheapoair.com

E-Cards

All 4 Free
An Internet greeting card index
www.rats2u.com

Hallmark.com
The online site of the popular card and gift store
www.hallmark.com

Blue Mountain
Popular cards available to send online
www.bluemountain.com

Other Interesting Sites

Smile by Webshots
A place to post photos for friends and family
http://smile.webshots.com

Facebook
An online directory connecting people through social networks at
colleges and beyond
www.facebook.com

Grub Hub
Online source for local restaurants that deliver
www.grubhub.com

Classmates.com
An online database of high school graduates
www.classmates.com

Doodle
Helps groups of people find shared availability for meetings, parties, etc.
www.doodle.com

Consumer Reports
A nonprofit organization and print magazine with product reviews and other information
www.consumerreports.org

Huffington Post
Breaking news and opinions
www.huffingtonpost.com

Strategic Timelines for Choosing a Major

No major guarantees a straight path to success, but if you've examined your choices carefully and picked a major that suits your passions and skills you should be able to progress, anticipate roadblocks, and navigate the crossroads. Wherever you are in your academic journey, here are some points to keep in mind.

High School Students

Think about majors and careers, but don't exaggerate the importance of identifying and declaring a major just yet. Explore your options beyond high school, including colleges, universities, community colleges, and professional training institutions. Add any schools that have majors that interest you, but don't overlook a school just because it doesn't offer a particular major. Look at each school's curriculum to see what prerequisite and required distributive courses it offers. Create your own top-twenty list of the courses you might want to take someday, and a top-five list of possible majors for each school to which you might apply.

College Freshmen

Take as much of a variety of courses as you can. If your school has prerequisite or required distributive courses, take any that you find intriguing to see if you might be interested in majoring in the subject area. Read course descriptions, and come up with ideas for courses you will take this semester as well as those you might take in the future.

You don't have to create an ideal schedule for all four years, but you should develop your list of top-twenty classes. Don't worry about whether these classes have prerequisites or are available to freshmen. Make a top-five list of majors as well. Note any patterns or trends in your lists. Begin to think about "What can I do *if* I major in _____?" and examine specific courses that would be required of the majors you're thinking about. By the end of your freshman year you should have a clear top five major list, in addition to a top-twenty course list. Don't forget that you can take courses over the summer, too.

Sophomores

Most of you will have to declare a major by the end of this year. Remember that you can change your mind later if you want to. Once you have a particular major in mind, consider if it would be useful to take an additional major, minor, cluster, certificate, or courses over the summer. The first semester of your sophomore year is the ideal time to create or update your top-twenty course list and top-five major list.

The summer between your sophomore and junior years is ideal for internships, shadowing (externships), or talking to people about majors and careers. These practical experiences will have an impact on your ability to prioritize career options and find jobs after college. If you need to, seek the help of career service professionals.

Juniors

Think about whether you want to change majors, add a minor or cluster, or begin a one-course-at-a-time strategy. During this year you should be prepared and able to state your post-baccalaureate graduate school and/or career goals concisely and with confidence. With these goals in mind, you can decide if you have the skills necessary to enter these fields or you need to acquire them. You should be looking for answers to "What can I do *with* my major?"

The summer between your junior and senior years is a crucial one for exploration and skills-building experiences, or internships. Consult your school's career-services office for internship search strategies, postings, internship-specific resources, and help creating the very best job-search documentation possible, including resumes and cover letters. Explore programs that can bridge the gap from your major to a career, including The Washington Center for Internships (*www.twc.edu*) a program that offers housing, internships, and education programs in diverse fields and settings in Washington, D.C.

Seniors

During the first semester of your senior year you should know "What I can do *with* my major." You should also know how your minor or selective courses enhance your potential for a successful job search. You need to be thinking about what you'll be doing next year—not necessarily for the rest of your life. If the answer involves graduate study, talk to career services professionals, faculty members, and any specialist advisors about step-by-step efforts, deadlines, and specialized testing. All of this should be done during the first semester. If it involves post-graduation employment only, or in addition to applications to graduate schools, you must do the research early that's required to set and articulate your goals so you can implement effective strategies throughout the year.

Don't forget the value of the one-course-at-a-time strategy. Once you know what you want to do, figure out if a course or two will enhance your potential to get interviews and job offers. Also think about internships during and even after your senior year. A post-baccalaureate internship can be a springboard to a desired job. Network with family, faculty, alumni, and others. Such networking can help you refine your goals, as well as yield advice and even referrals. And don't forget to take advantage of the resources offered by your school's career services office.

Internet Resources for Finding a Major

Your school's career center and library both contain a great deal of helpful information on choosing a major. While career counselors and reference librarians are professionals trained to help you locate resources for choosing a major, you can do a lot of preliminary research online. Here is a list of some of the most valuable online resources.

www.online.onetcenter.org
Users select existing skills and those they plan to develop to identify careers that typically use those skills.

www.careerexplorer.net
Offers a Motivational Appraisal of Personal Potential (MAPP) test that focuses on motivation and corresponding talents.

www.careerkey.org
Contains links and assessments that measure values, interests, personality, and skills.

www.collegeboard.com
The Majors & Careers Central site helps you explore options and identify schools that match your specific needs.

www.discoveryourpersonality.com
The original Myers-Briggs and other career assessments. Provides live follow-up consultations by phone.

www.iseek.org
Includes an exercise that links skills with occupational interests and education-related information.

www.livecareer.com
Identifies career interests and matches them to job functions and careers.

www.similarminds.com
Personality test site and community that offers several options.

www.testingroom.com
A site dedicated to self-assessment, with links to numerous online tests and assessments addressing values and personality traits.

www.typefocus.com
Provides a free Myers-Briggs inspired assessment and other instruments for a fee.

www.vault.com and *www.wetfeet.com*
Two data-laden sites offering advice on job searching and information on career fields and potential employers.

Index

Academic advisers, 136–37
Academic websites, 230
Admissions office, 32
Advisement, 136–37
Air conditioning, 123
Air freshener, 127
All 4 Free, 236
Allmovie, 234
Allmusic, 234
Alternative spring break websites, 230
Alumni, 33, 219–20
Amazon.com, 234
American College Personnel Association (ACPA), 220
Angelfire, 232
Anxiety, 163
Athletic department, 33
ATMs, 117–18

Banks, 115–18
Bank statements, 119
Barnes and Noble, 234
Bathroom essentials, 77–79
Bedding, 77
Bibliographies, 186–89
Bigwords, 234
Bills, 58–59
Blue Mountain, 236
Body, of paper, 205–08
Bored.com, 232
Brainstorming, 198–99
Break Away, 230
Brochures, 17
Budgets, 120–24

Calendar, 158–61
Calendar systems, 164–65
Campus jobs, 46–47
Campus safety, 62–63
Campus visits, 18–29
Card Act, 112
Career centers, 144, 220
Career fairs, 220–21
Car insurance, 75
Cash, 110
Cash advances, 113, 114
Catalogs
    college, 17
    library, 182, 185–86
Cell phones, 122
Center for Students with Disabilities, 66
Cheapo Air, 235
Checkbooks, balancing, 118–19
Checks, 111
Chegg.com, 234
Chegg.com's Homework Help, 230
Citations, 183, 211
Class discussions, 171
Classes
    minimizing distractions during, 172
    note taking in, 170–72
Classmates.com, 236
Class selection, 135–243
Cleaning, 125–27
Cleaning supplies, 77, 127
Clothing, 77, 81–84
Clustering, 198
CMJ, 233
Cold calling, 221

College
    cost vs. value of, 50–52
    experience of, 11–13
    preparing for, 57–72
    websites, 16–17
College brochures and catalogs, 17
College finances, 39–56. *See also*
    Financial aid
College guides, 16
College Humor, 231
College selection process, 15–37
    campus visits, 18–29
    information sources, 16–18
    near vs. far away colleges,
        30–32
Computerized information
    resources, 188–89
Conclusion, of paper, 208–09
Consumer Reports, 237
Core requirements, 141–43
Cost vs. value, 50–52
Coupons, 123
Cover letters, 218
Cramming sessions, 166
Credit cards, 111–15
Credit rating, 113–15
Credit reports, 114–15

Debit cards, 111
Decorations, 77, 85
Doodle, 237
Dorm rooms
    changing, 105–07
    keeping clean, 125–27
    making it feel like home, 84–87
    moving in to, 99–101

moving out of, 89–90
packing for, 74–84
and roommates, 91–107
Double major, 147–48
Drafts
    revising, 209–11
    writing first, 201–02
Dry cleaners, 134
Dryer safety, 131

EasyJet.com, 235
eBaum's World, 231
E-cards, 236
Education, cost vs. value of, 50–52
Educational loans, 48–50
efollet, 234
Employment, 46–47, 159–60
Entertainment expenses, 122
Essays. *See also* Papers
    proofreading, 212–13
    researching, 181–96
    revising, 209–11
    structuring, 202–09
    writing, 197–213
Exams
    cramming for, 166
    studying for, 158–59, 161, 166,
        169–79
Expedia Travel, 235

Facebook, 236
Fans, 77
FARK.com, 231
Federal Perkins Loans, 48
Federal Stafford Loans, 48

Financial aid
  forms, 40–41
  grants, 41–44
  leadership development
    awards, 45–46
  loans, 48–50
  offices, 40–41
  questions about, 34
  scholarships, 41–44
  sources of, 51
  studying abroad and, 149
  tracker, 52–56
  work-study aid, 46–47
Financial materials, 58–59
Finding Dulcinea, 230
First drafts
  revising, 209–11
  writing, 201–02
Flash cards, 176–77
Flu vaccinations, 60
Foreign language classes, 143
Foreign study, 148–55
Free Application for Federal Student Aid (FAFSA), 41
Free time, 160–61
Freewriting, 198
Freshmen, 240–41
Friends
  as information choice, 17–18
  making new, 70
Furniture, 74–75

Games, online, 231–32
Grammar checkers, 211, 213
Grants, 41–44
Grub Hub, 236

Habits, 169
Half.com, 234
Hallmark.com, 236
Health center, 60–61
Health insurance, 59–62
Health services office, 32
High school students, 240
Homeowner's insurance, 62
Homestarrunner, 232
Home visits, 36
Hostels Worldwide, 235
Housing, 63–66
Housing office, 32
Huffington Post, 237
Hulu, 233
Humor web sites, 231–32

Idea generation, 198–99
IMDb, 233
Immunization records, 60, 61
Independence, 36
Index cards, 183, 193–95
Indexes, 186–89
Information sources, for choosing a college, 16–18
Insurance
  for belongings, 62–63
  car, 75
  health, 59–62
Interlibrary loans, 182
Internet resources, 229–37, 245–47
Internet searches, 183, 189
Internship directories, 221
Internships
  basics of, 217–19
  definition of, 216

finding, 219–25
  interviewing for, 218–19
  paid, 216–17
  post-baccalaureate, 243
  reflecting on, 226–27
  summer, 215–27, 241–42
Intersession programs, 151
Interviews, 218–19
Introduction, 203–05

Jewish National Fund, 230
JibJab, 231
Jobs. *See also* Internships
  campus, 46–47
  summer, 159–60
Juniors, 241–42

Keepsakes, 86

Lastminute.com, 235
Laundry, 128–34, 163
Laundry services, 133
Laundry supplies, 77
Leadership development awards,
  45–46
Learning communities, 65–66
Legacy Trap, 18
Librarians, 189
Library, 182, 185, 189
Library catalog, 182, 185–86
Lighting, 77
Lint filters, 131
Livejournal, 232
Live United, 230

Loans, 48–50
Local banks, 115–18
Locker, 63

Mad Blast, 231
Major
  declaring a, 144–47
  double, 147–48
  Internet resources for finding,
    245–47
  timeline for choosing, 239–43
Master calendar, 158–61
Medications, 78–79
Mental health, 163
Milk and Cookies, 232
Mini Clip, 231
Minors, 147–48
Movie websites, 233–34
Moving, 73–90, 99–101
Multitasking, 162–63
Music websites, 233–34

Netflix, 233
Note cards, 193–95
Note taking
  in class, 170–72
  during research, 191–95

Office of Civil Rights (OCR), 67
Office supplies, 173
The Onion, 231
Online catalogs, 185–86
Online resources, 183, 188–89,
  245–47

Online shopping, 76, 122–23
Online time management tools, 165
Orbitz Travel, 235
Organization tips, 172–74
Orientation, 67–71
Orientation office, 33, 68
Outlines, 199–201
OVG, 233

Packing, 74–84
Pajamas, 83
Papers
    body of, 205–08
    conclusion, 208–09
    first drafts, 201–02
    introduction, 203–05
    length of, 210–11
    plagiarism and, 190, 193, 195–96
    planning, 198–201
    proofreading, 212–13
    researching, 181–96
    structuring, 202–09
    writing, 197–213
Paragraphs
    flow between, 208
    focusing on specific point, 208
    length of, 207
Paraphrasing, 191–93, 206
Parents
    changing relationship with, 34–37
    loans for, 49
Passport, 120
Payments, records of, 58
Perkins Loans, 48

Personal finances, 109–24
    balancing checkbook, 118–19
    budgeting, 120–24
    cash, 110
    checks, 111
    credit cards, 111–15
    debit cards, 111
    local banks, 115–18
    safety precautions, 119–20
    school charge card, 110
Petty theft, 62–63
Pharmacies, 60
Photographs, 85–86
Physicals, 59
Plagiarism, 190, 193, 195–96
Planners, 164–65
PLUS program, 49
Pollstar, 233
Posters, 85
Pre-orientation programs, 69–70
Primary sources, 184
Professional organizations, 220
Proofreading, 212–13

Questions
    about loans, 49–50
    to ask during campus visits, 20–21
    to ask roommate, 94–96
    interview, 218–19
    at orientation, 70
    while reading, 178–79
    who to contact with, 32–34
Quotations, 191–92, 205, 206

Rate My Professor, 230
Reading skills, 177–79
Relationships
    with parents, 34–37
    with roommates, 98–99
    staying connected, 34–37
Relatives
    as information source, 17–18
    staying connected with, 34
Research, 181–96
    conducting, 182–83
    Internet, 183, 189
    note taking, 191–95
    plagiarism and, 190, 193, 195–96
    process, 184–85
    tracking sources, 183, 190, 194
    where to find sources, 185–89
Reserve Officers' Training Corps
    (ROTC), 46
Residence halls, 65–66, 74–87. *See
    also* Dorm rooms
Resident assistants (RAs), 105
Resumes, 218
Roommates, 91–107
    agreements with, 101–04
    building relationship with,
        98–99
    conflicts with, 96, 98–99, 102,
        104–07
    meeting, 93–97
    questionnaire, 63–65
    room changes and, 105–07
    room cleaning and, 126–27
    selection, 92–93
Rough drafts. *See* First drafts
Rule of Three, 199

Safety
    on campus, 62–63
    dryer, 131
    money, 119–20
Safety deposit box, 63
Schedules
    class, 138–40
    time, 158–59, 160–62
Scholarship databases, 42–43
Scholarships, 41–44
School charge card, 110
School supplies, 77
Secondary sources, 184–85
Self-discipline, 162
Seniors, 242–43
Shoes, 83
Shopping, 122–23
Sidereel, 233
Smart phones, 165
Smile by Webshots, 236
Social media, 94
Sophomores, 241
Sources
    including in body of paper, 206
    keeping track of, 183, 190, 194
    primary, 184
    secondary, 184–85
    where to find, 185–89
Southwest Airlines, 235
Space savers, 78
Sparknotes, 230
Spell checkers, 213
Sporkle, 231
Spring break websites, 230
Stafford Loans, 48
Stain removal, 131–32, 134
Storage lockers, 89–90

Stress, 163
Student Affairs Administrators in Higher Education (NASPA), 220
Student ID, 120
Students with disabilities, 66–67
Student Universe, 235
Study groups, 174–75
Studying abroad, 148–55
Study skills, 169–79
  flash cards, 176–77
  note taking, 170–72
  organization tips, 172–74
  reading skills, 177–79
  summary, 179
Study space, organizing your, 173–74
Study time, 158–59, 161, 166
Stumble upon, 231
Style guides, 183
Subsidized loans, 48
Summer jobs, 215–17, 226–27. See also Internships
Summer programs, 151
Summer storage, 89–90
Summer vacation, 215, 226–27

Tax returns, 40–41
Textbooks, 123, 234
Theft, 62–63
Thesis statement, 203–05, 208
Time management, 157–67
  checklist, 167
  cramming, 166
  master calendar, 158–61
  multitasking, 162–63
  tools, 164–65
  trading time blocks, 161–62

Topic sentences, 208
Transitional words and phrases, 208
Transportation expenses, 124
Travel websites, 235
TV Duck, 233

Unscheduled events, 160–61
Unsubsidized loans, 48–49

Vaccinations, 59, 60, 61
Vacuums, 77, 127
Volunteer work, 226

Washing machines, 129, 130, 131
Webs.com, 232
Websites
  college, 16–17
  for college students, 229–37
  internship, 221
Wikipedia, 189
Works cited, 188, 194
Work-study aid, 46–47
WorldCat, 182
Writing process, 197–213
  first drafts, 201–02
  outlines, 199–201
  paper structure, 202–09
  planning, 198–201
  proofreading, 212–13
  revising, 209–11

Xanga.com, 232